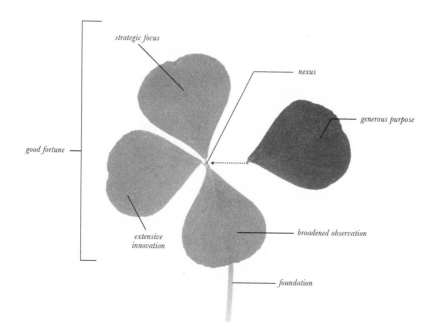

strategic focus

nexus

generous purpose

good fortune

extensive
innovation

broadened observation

foundation

Earning
Serendipity

4 SKILLS *for* CREATING *and* SUSTAINING GOOD FORTUNE *in* YOUR WORK

GLENN LLOPIS

GREENLEAF
BOOK GROUP PRESS

Published by Greenleaf Book Group Press
Austin, TX
www.greenleafbookgroup.com

Distributed by Greenleaf Book Group LLC

For ordering information or special discounts for bulk purchases, please contact Greenleaf Book Group LLC at PO Box 91869, Austin, TX 78709, (512) 891-6100.

Design and composition by Greenleaf Book Group LLC
Cover design by Greenleaf Book Group LLC

Publisher's Cataloging-in-Publication Data
(Prepared by The Donohue Group, Inc.)

Llopis, Glenn.
    Earning serendipity : four skills for creating and sustaining good fortune in your work / Glenn Llopis. -- 1st ed.

    p. ; cm.

    ISBN-13: 978-1-929774-91-3
    ISBN-10: 1-929774-91-5

1. Success in business. 2. Success--Life skills guides. 3. Self-actualization (Psychology) 4. Serendipity. I. Title.

HF5386 .L56 2009
650.1   2008941988

Part of the Tree Neutral™ program, which offsets the number of trees consumed in the production and printing of this book by taking proactive steps, such as planting trees in direct proportion to the number of trees used: www.treeneutral.com

TreeNeutral

Printed in the United States of America on acid-free paper

09 10 11 12 13 14   10 9 8 7 6 5 4 3 2 1

First Edition

DEDICATION

The words of this book began to be written on October 5, 1966. This is the day I was born into your arms. Since that day, you have always guided me rightly. You gave me a path and the tools to understand the complexities of life. The results were discoveries of hope, inspiration, and belief in myself. You taught me to trust *my* brand and to share it with others (with no scorecard attached). You gave life and meaning to my immigrant perspective. You wired me to not fear but rather seek my deepest desires. You taught me how to challenge the status quo responsibly for the betterment of all. You gave me the eyes to navigate the obstacles and with each, discover new adventures. Your teachings made me realize that business is a civic responsibility, that enterprise is about the advancement of people not brands, and that brands serve as identifiers and society builders. With all you have taught me, I seek to make these things so.

Dad, thank you for enlightening me with your soul, your wisdom, and your treasured discoveries. With your permission and in your honor, the education that transpired from our indescribable relationship will now be shared responsibly with society. Your lessons have prepared me to lead in a world of uncertainty and to reshape it. They taught me to discover my own purpose and develop a methodology to propel innovation in business and in everyday life. As such, in your name, I shall now embark upon my own journey: to lead a movement to propel innovation the world over. You trained me to inspire, mentor, and teach others. This is what I set off to do for the rest of my life, but the task at hand demands more than just me. As you have taught me, my journey is a quest to meet and discover people who seek responsible innovation and desire the discipline to see, sow, grow, and share the harvest of their good fortune. I call these people "serendipiters," and it is now my duty to help unite business and society to build a community of serendipiters that stands for a common language and breeds global innovation. I can only hope that the momentum of my earned serendipity will connect me with influential leaders in business, government, and society who will help me propel the awareness and creation of this serendipiters community. But don't worry, Dad, I will forever pass on, for generations to come, your lessons and inherent wisdom. You are the ultimate serendipiter!

As I close this dedication to you, I will share your favorite Spanish proverb because I promised you that this book would convey its message hidden within each chapter.

El vivo vive del bobo y el bobo de su trabajo.—The wise one lives off the fool and the fool lives off his job.

Dad, you are my hero and guiding light. I will continue to serve as your proud son, a devoted husband and father, and a highly responsible citizen of society. Thank you for teaching me how to live wisely and allow others to join me. With all of my love, Glenn.

Those that earn serendipity
see what others don't,
do what others won't,
and keep pushing when prudence says quit.

CONTENTS

* *We have skipped two chapters, for the one who learns to create and
sustain a momentum of good fortune possesses the power to leap ahead.*

FOREWORD

You may not know it until you read this book, but you have just earned serendipity. You bought this book.

The concept of earning serendipity, on its surface, seems internally inconsistent. How can one earn luck? But as Glenn explains, serendipity is not pure luck.

Prior to becoming a professor, I spent eighteen years as a Wall Street investment banker, followed by seven years running a major homeless agency in Los Angeles. During my career, I have met many successful—and unsuccessful—people. And at the surface, the successful ones often appear luckier than those who didn't achieve success. (You will note that I don't use *wealthy* and *poor* here—those words are not always the best measures of success.)

But as I learned more about both groups, I came to understand that what looked like pure serendipity was actually the result of a better understanding of how the world worked. The successful folks seemed to be able to see things and put things together in a different manner. It appeared as though they had some secret—a method of becoming "lucky." However, it wasn't until I met Glenn and he explained his methodology that I realized that what truly successful people knew was how to *earn* that serendipity.

When I first met Glenn, I knew within a few minutes that he was someone who not only had achieved success but also understood the methodology of earning it. The better I got to know Glenn, the more I was convinced that he belonged to a rare breed. Glenn was able to clearly articulate how what appeared serendipitous was actually the result of a different way of viewing the world and therefore of living in it. He was able to map out the steps, explain the process, and communicate clearly. But most amazing, he was willing and eager to share his methods.

"How can that be?" I asked Glenn. Many of those who appeared successful on the surface viewed the world as a zero-sum game—in order for *me* to win, *you* have to lose. Why would Glenn, an obviously successful person, be willing to let others in on his secrets? The answer, he explained, was that "sharing his harvest" was actually one of the steps to achieving success in the first place! Lucky us!

Last year, I opened the Society and Business Lab at the Marshall School of Business at the University of Southern California. We were responding to a trend in business toward what has come to be known as Corporate Social Responsibility. Responding to a demand from consumers, investors, and employees, corporations were called upon to be more transparent and to act more responsibly. There would no longer be any patience for multinational corporations ruining the environment, abusing labor, and ignoring the communities where they did business. Even more important, the new generation of corporate leaders seemed to be more self-aware and to understand their societal roles clearly. I opened the Lab to develop new models for the large businesses to act as better citizens of the world.

Glenn innately understands this responsibility and is able to take it to the level of the current or would-be entrepreneur. But

Glenn explains that rather than following the traditional model of first becoming successful and then becoming socially responsible, it works another way: Sharing the harvest is a major factor—a part of the process—in becoming successful in the first place. According to Glenn, it also requires looking at the world in a new way and maneuvering through that world in a determined and structured manner. There is actually a way to earn serendipity.

My brother Elon, may he rest in peace, was an oral surgeon with a successful practice in New York. When other dentists and oral surgeons interviewed to work in his practice, he would ask them all the same question: "Do you consider yourself lucky?" My brother innately knew that the people who considered themselves "lucky" had actually earned their serendipity. The world of surgery, just like the business world, required looking at things the way most people didn't, preparing a path of focused learning and apprentice-ship, and making sure that patients felt cared for. So if you wanted to get a job working in my brother's successful practice, you should have met Glenn.

And now, by reading this book and following Glenn's methods, you, too, will be successful—you will earn serendipity.

—Adlai Wertman
    Professor of Clinical Management and Organization
    Founding Director, Society and Business Lab
    Marshall School of Business at the University of Southern California

THE FOUNDATION

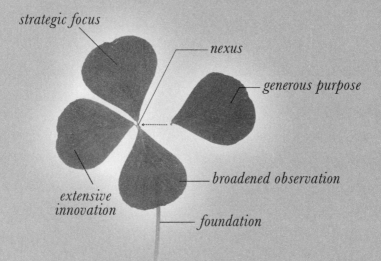

strategic focus

nexus

generous purpose

extensive innovation

broadened observation

foundation

foundation

CHAPTER 0

Creating and Sustaining Good Fortune in Your Work

"Only learn to seize good fortune, for good fortune is always here."
—JOHANN WOLFGANG VON GOETHE

I make only one promise: your life will not be the same. What I offer is more than advice, more than hope. I offer you a mirror. In it you will see you are more powerful than you know. I offer you a map. With it you will discover you are closer than you know to a career of good fortune.

You've heard it said that chance governs us all, but I tell you that fortune is not arbitrary. There are the lucky: the lottery winners filing for bankruptcy, the gamblers betting away their winnings, the trust fund babies trapped in apathy. They know nothing of good fortune. Their lives are grains of sand slave to the ebbing and flowing tide, sand castles for only an hour.

Then there are the flourishing: those who outlive, outwork, and out love—to whom good things always seem to come. They inhabit a foundation from which positive happenstance seems to grow in abundance. Yet their good fortune springs not from mere chance but from the rare abilities to see what the majority miss and to exploit what most think uncontrollable. They are not lucky, and their fortune is no accident.

It is said that misfortune chases us all, but I tell you that fortune pursues you more swiftly. It reaches for you. You must learn only to seize it where it dwells—in the obvious and obscure places all around you—and to sow its seeds wherever you go. I will give you the eyes to see good fortune and the tools to keep it on your side from this day forward.

ALL YOU HAVE NOT YET SEEN

There is more happening around you than you might realize. It is said that you find what you are looking for, but I tell you that if you learn to look around and beyond what you seek, you will discover things more valuable, timely, and true. Perhaps I am being too mystical. Or perhaps I am confirming something you've sensed all along.

I am speaking of serendipity—what some call "positive happenstance." Most believe it comes capriciously, without hint of how, when, or why. The jobless woman takes lunch alone in Central Park on a cool autumn day. As she picks at her bland leftovers, a businesswoman approaches to ask for directions, and in an instant, a connection is made and her dream job is found.

We like to say she was lucky . . . or that the universe had mercy on her . . . or that it was a matter of finally being in the right place at the right time.

But what if it was more than a chance occurrence? What if I told you she'd been undervalued by her former employer for years . . . and that she'd finally left the company and moved to Manhattan to forge a new path . . . and that she'd always loved autumn in New York and especially in Central Park? Perhaps such observations would expand your notion about what happened and whether she had some control over her good fortune.

With a rare combination of four skills, you will begin to see and seize the momentous opportunities around you before they have passed you by. Opportunities of which you were not previously aware—often, the only opportunities that will enlarge your career path and increase your propensity for success and fulfillment every day. Most are blind to these opportunities, and this is the primary reason so many workers are uninspired, merely putting in time to meet unremarkable goals.

It has been said that self-knowledge is the mother of success, but success is first born of something else. Self-knowledge is the offspring of experience—we learn of ourselves through that which our senses take in—and experience is the offspring of the opportunities we have pursued.

Opportunity is the true mother of success.

Opportunity is the primary catalyst for sustaining good fortune in your career or company. And it builds momentum quicker than any other success factor.

One right opportunity skillfully pursued births a host of additional opportunities that would otherwise have never existed. A middle manager steps off the corporate track to launch an online venture with a close friend. With a little money and a lot of heart, the two succeed in putting their business on the map in the first year. The business multiplies exponentially the following year and is featured in two major publications—one a cover story. In the third year, this once-small venture garners a large offer from a Web-based giant. The acquisition not only opens the doors to a host of new business ventures, it also initiates requests for both partners to consult large organizations on how to differentiate Web presence and small organizations on how to establish Web presence. The former middle manager also receives a sizable advance for a forthcoming book.

Three years earlier, there was a middle manager with a predictable paycheck and an inside track to a corner office in ten years. Perhaps not a bad career path, but certainly not what it could be. With one opportunity seen and seized rightly, the individual enlarged the field before him and changed his fortune forever. With the subsequent opportunities that bloomed, he then created a momentum of good fortune that was his to preserve. The same is available to you. You must only learn to see and grow opportunities rightly.

The significance and impact of your work has more to do with the momentum of opportunities you pursue than anything else. The quantity of opportunities is a smaller matter. The quality of opportunities is everything. This explains why a green twentysomething can birth Facebook while fortysomethings everywhere struggle to make ends meet—or why more people became millionaires during the Great Depression than during any other era of American history, including the dot-com boom.

*Opportunities are always present, and rightly pursuing one
can forever change the landscape of one's fortune.*

The opportunities you see and grow determine the fortune of your career or corporate venture. Self-knowledge can give you insight. Experience can give you confidence. But the two are tamed without the right opportunities. One right opportunity pursued can elevate the potential of any career and any organization.

THE SCIENCE OF GOOD FORTUNE

We speak of things like "overnight success" and "a stroke of luck" as though they are shrouded in mystery. I will show you that most changes in fortune—those outside of betting luck—are no mystery at all. They are the result of a rare combination of four skills employed on a regular basis. Not every fortunate person is aware she is employing these activities, which explains why most experience good fortune only rarely and randomly. But those who learn to employ the quartet on a regular basis discover a reservoir of power greater than self-knowledge, greater than intuition, and greater than experience. And they thus tap into a reservoir of potential most never reach. The ability to earn serendipity will elevate a career or company quicker than any single force. If sustained well, it yields a tradition of success.

At times we witness one who seems to be in the midst of a lucky streak. But what appears to be one opportunity, one windfall, one great experience after another is actually the natural by-product of certain skills applied on a continual basis.

You see, serendipity is not governed by chance alone. I must concede there is an art to good fortune—certain occurrences cannot be fully explained or controlled. A middle-aged couple strolls through a Vegas casino on their way to meet friends for dinner. On a whim, the husband slides one quarter into a slot machine and hits a six-figure jackpot. We speak of his "good fortune," but such inexplicable occurrences are better deemed "luck." While they occur every day all over the world, they can be neither controlled nor explained. At best, we can appreciate them. But to lean on such lucky breaks—to lean on the art of good fortune—is no strategy at all. It is merely far-fetched hope. The odds of success are never in your favor.

However, there is also a science to good fortune. It can be earned, not by will, force, or manipulation, but by the application of four skills to your workdays. This rare blend of skills taps into an immense power that few ever take the time to understand, let alone master. Yet those that do hold sway not only in the workplace but also in society at large. I call the four skills the Four Leaves, and together they represent an uncommon crop—a propensity for good fortune that, when well managed, yields a tradition of success with opportunities perpetually budding. These Four Leaves are

1. Broadened Observation: The practice of seeing with circular vision

2. Extensive Innovation: The practice of sowing entrepreneurial seeds

3. Strategic Focus: The practice of growing seeds of greatest potential

4. Generous Purpose: The practice of sharing the harvest

I call the one who makes regular use of the Four Leaves a *serendipiter*: a socially conscious individual, or organization, who inspires innovation and initiative and thus propels good fortune for himself and his community. Applied daily, the Four Leaves expand the field of opportunities before you and all serendipiters, increasing your leverage, your influence, and your propensity for success. The Earning Serendipity Methodology plays out visually as shown in figure 1. It teaches a unique combination of entrepreneurial skills that yield a progressive workplace brimming with innovation and initiative.

The process of earning serendipity is very simple to understand when you assume the perspective of an immigrant. There is a reason we call the United States "the land of opportunity," but it is the immigrant who knows this better than anyone.

Figure 1: The Earning Serendipity Methodology

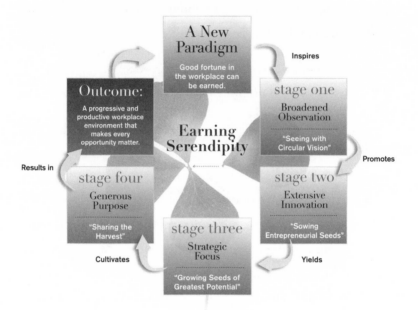

He comes to America with nothing but faith and hope, and he consequently views everything as opportunity. He is neither myopic nor careless in his pursuits but rather sees every relationship, every job, every dollar, and every day through the lens of potential. He thus sows entrepreneurial seeds wherever he goes—in people, in jobs, in new ventures and experiences—not knowing for certain which seeds will sprout but trusting that the more he sows, the greater the potential harvest. Some of his seeds sprout immediately—perhaps he is given a job that brings him a good income or perhaps he is given a loan to begin a business of his own. He cultivates these seeds through focus to ensure they grow to their potential. All the while, he continues sowing other seeds everywhere he goes. In time, something begins to happen—something we might call luck had we no knowledge of the man's habits: seedlings begin to spring up all around him.

> *Generous favors blossom into friendships.*
> *Odd jobs blossom into annual contracts.*
> *Coworkers blossom into supporters.*
> *Bosses blossom into advocates.*
> *Friends blossom into partners.*
> *Ideas blossom into enterprises.*

Perhaps it seems the man is charmed. Opportunities spring from everywhere he looks. But did he not earn the growing harvest before him? Is not the increased income merely the fruit of his labor? Has he not earned the equity in relationships and leverage in enterprise?

It is so. And his harvest will continue to grow as he continues on this path. I must tell you, however, the rare combination of skills with which the man earned his serendipity is only potent as a quartet.

Many possess one or two of the Four Leaves in good measure. A select few possess three. Such individuals will experience good fortune in random spurts, but they will not produce a predictable, perpetual harvest. I will explain what I mean.

While one might gain a greater measure of advancement and success from (1) seeing with circular vision the best opportunities before him, one will not reap good fortune without also (2) sowing entrepreneurial seeds into each opportunity. We call those with the gift of keen observation "visionaries" or "idea people." They are brimming with suggestions for solution and advancement, yet they must rely on others to initiate action.

Furthermore, one may possess the skill to (1) see opportunities and (2) sow entrepreneurial seeds but then lack the skill to (3) grow seeds of greatest potential through focus. She, too, will not consistently earn good fortune. We call her a "go-getter" or a "self-starter." She is self-motivated and ambitious yet lacking in endurance. We appoint her to frontline selling but require other positions to complete the path to success.

And then a very small number will (1) see opportunities, (2) sow entrepreneurial seeds, and then (3) grow seeds of greatest potential through focus. Such people will climb high—they will lead divisions and launch companies and important ventures. Yet if they do not set out to (4) share their harvest with others, they will not sustain a momentum of good fortune. They will reap success, but the success will not multiply as it could. You have no doubt observed the rising stock of this fourth skill all around you—corporations call it "social responsibility" and individuals call it a "cause." Perhaps we are beginning to understand.

The one who employs the quartet of skills on a regular basis will find no shortage of good fortune throughout his or her career. Yet this momentum of good fortune is also sustainable for the organization that employs people skilled in each of the four arenas. And it is in this way—through the strategic employment of people skilled in (1) seeing opportunities, (2) sowing seeds, (3) growing seeds, and (4) sharing success—that an organization of any size will reap a perpetual harvest of good fortune.

There are thus two ways in which you might read this book:

1. As an individual who aspires to ensure a momentum of good fortune in your work

2. As a company that aspires to ensure a momentum of good fortune throughout the organization

To help you maintain both perspectives I offer profiles of people and organizations who have lived the Earning Serendipity Methodology: Amazon.com and Jeff Bezos, Costco, Google and Larry Page and Sergey Brin, and IKEA. These profiles are presented after each leaf is explained. Finally, I conclude with the ultimate serendipiter—Thomas Edison.

PREPARING FOR GREATER POSSIBILITIES

To create and sustain the momentum of good fortune—to earn serendipity—one must regularly employ the quartet of skills: (1) seeing the best opportunities, (2) sowing entrepreneurial seeds, (3) growing seeds through focus, and (4) sharing the eventual harvest. This practice of earning serendipity, my father once explained, is not governed merely by corporate laws but also by universal laws like attraction, responsibility, and reciprocity. The effectiveness of earning serendipity is not measured merely by unique visitors, volume, and profits but also by influence, compassion, and impact. Its time is not bound by nine-to-five but by birth and death. My father would conclude,

"¿Ahora, que ve ante usted?"— Now, what do you see before you?

It is the same question I ask you now. What might your work look like if you possessed the skills to regularly see, sow, grow, and share the best opportunities before you? What might your company look like if your people embodied these four skills on a daily basis?

What you have missed is no matter now. What you must consider today are the discoveries yet before you. I assure you, some are already within reach. With the proper sight, your present can look quite different. With the proper skills, your future will change forever.

History sides with what I say.

An apple fell from a tree and a man saw something more than bothersome fruit. Isaac Newton saw an expanded theory of gravity.

A torsion spring fell from a worktable and a naval officer saw more than a clumsy spill. Richard James saw a Slinky.

A rubber compound spilled onto a tennis shoe and a chemist saw more than a stubborn stain. Patsy Sherman saw Scotchgard, a spill to protect against all spills.

A moldy culture of bacteria sat forgotten in a laboratory, yet a scientist saw more than dirty equipment. Alexander Fleming saw penicillin.

It is no coincidence that those to whom keen observation was second nature were those who historically made momentous, life-changing discoveries. Scientists are trained to look beyond the obvious. Explorers like Ericsson and Columbus have eyes to see more than what is expected. Such people know that while looking for a route to one country, one might discover something else entirely: a whole other country with a whole other set of opportunities. Perhaps now it makes sense to you that it was a famous chemist, Louis

Pasteur, who said, "In the fields of observation, chance only favors the prepared mind." For certain, Pasteur was referring to the sciences. But is not the marketplace also a "field of observation"? It is. And in the world of enterprise, it is equally true that fortune favors those who are prepared to find it.

POWER AND RESPONSIBILITY

My father once asserted,

> "Remember, most people only work. You must learn to flourish and then you must teach others to do the same."

When I heard this, I knew it was from uncommon wisdom that he spoke. I was raised in no typical fashion. Earning serendipity has been to me a reality from the beginning—from the first time my father spoke it to my boyish ears. Today, it alters every aspect of my life: my work ethic, my business plans, my relationships, and my investment of resources. It allowed me to become the youngest senior manager in the 100-plus-year history of Sunkist and, a few years later, the 30-year-old vice president of the billion-dollar Norway Seafood Company. The practice of earning serendipity allowed me to then launch my first entrepreneurial endeavor a year later, and since then I have launched seven companies, with products and services sold in five countries.

Much of what I know, I was taught. Some, I inherited. We Cubans are resilient, opportunistic people. We love life and are wired for the pursuit of revolutionary ideas and nonnegotiable ideals. Fused together, the characteristics make us potent pioneers of good fortune. Born of this mold are fellow Cuban Americans like Robert Goizueta, former CEO of Coca-Cola; Carlos Gutierrez, former CEO of Kellogg and U.S. Secretary of Commerce; Nelson Gonzalez and Alex Aquila, founders of Alienware; Gedalio Grinberg, founder and CEO of Movado watches; and Samuel Palmisano, CEO of IBM. So too is my mother, Jenny Llopis, a prominent model and dancer during the famed Havana nights. And so too is my father, Frank Llopis.

After being forced from his beloved homeland by Castro's revolution, my father went on to become one of the most renowned Cuban musicians of his time, with Beatles-like fame throughout Spain, Mexico, and Central and South America. His quartet, Los Llopis, is known as the first to blend the capricious rhythms of salsa and merengue with American rock-and-roll. The quartet is still mentioned in the same breath as legends like Celia Cruz and Beny Moré.

To say my father knew the right opportunity when he saw it is an understatement. My father seemed to see opportunities for which no one else had eyes—some, in fact, that many considered counterproductive. Yet his good fortune continued long after his music career. At forty-nine years old, my father returned to his first love, chemical engineering. He moved to Azusa, California, where he went on to become one of the chemists responsible for the creation of Miller Lite. You might say he was one of the first to live the High Life.

Today Frank Llopis is ninety-three and still seeing and growing the good fortune all around him. His body is weak yet his voice still spills confidence and conviction. He is my hero and greatest teacher, but now it is I who remind him of his words to me as a boy. He challenged me to write this book to tell others what we have learned. I challenged him to learn five new songs on his guitar by Christmas. He will learn ten.

I share this personal history with you so you might comprehend that earning serendipity is more than a work or business strategy. It is also a heritage passed down through generations, and with heritage comes responsibility. I speak of the responsibility you have to yourself to realize the potential that is within you—you are more powerful than you know. I speak also of the responsibility you have to humanity. With a momentum of good fortune comes obligation. I can only teach you the skills to take hold of good fortune. It will then be up to you to master the skills and put them to best use—for more than your fortune alone—for the fortunes of others as well. May it be your ultimate goal as we now begin this momentous journey.

THE FOUR LEAVES

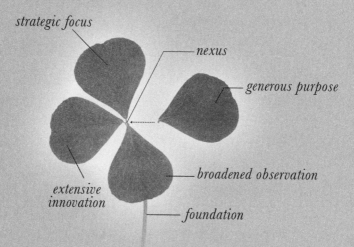

strategic focus

nexus

generous purpose

extensive innovation

broadened observation

foundation

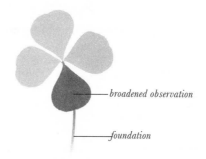

broadened observation

foundation

CHAPTER 1

Broadened Observation: *Seeing* with Circular Vision

"It is we that are blind, not fortune."

—SIR THOMAS BROWNE

Growing up with roots in both the United States and Cuba, I received a diverse education in culture and enterprise. Many important lessons arose from this upbringing, but none was more important to my career than an observation I made in my early twenties. It is this: In America, you can be an entrepreneur; in Latin America, you must be.

While my first job with the Gallo Wine Companies presented me with great opportunities to climb the sturdy American corporate ladder, my Cuban roots pointed my eyes toward opportunity everywhere I looked—inside and outside the company. They exposed my eyes to not only what was before me but also what was around, beneath, and beyond what was plain to see. I learned this skill from my father, a man who continually discovered opportunity in unfamiliar lands.

During the 1930s, my father had the opportunity to attend high school in the United States. He attended Massanutten Military Academy in Woodstock, Virginia. It was there that he looked beyond the obvious and saw the opportunity to apply his knowledge of the sciences. He created a dark room in the small confines of his dorm room and established a business developing black-and-white photography. His fellow students preferred the better value they received from the dorm-room lab than from the local photography lab. My father had the broadened observation to see an opportunity and then sow and grow its seeds.

After graduation, my father first attended the Massachusetts Institute of Technology and then transferred to Cornell University to obtain a degree in chemical engineering. With a degree in hand, he returned to Cuba where he worked as a chemist for a few industry giants, such as Colgate-Palmolive. But my father was not content to follow the obvious opportunities before him. His passion was music, and at the age of thirty-nine he launched his famous quartet. This opportunity taken allowed him to meet dancer Jenny Léon, the woman who would become my mother.

The popularity of the band grew in the next few years, and six months after Castro's revolution unfolded, my mom and dad began touring with Los Llopis. He traveled everywhere, sowing seeds of optimism and hope. He still shares many rich friendships with those his music touched. To this day, I still meet people who were impacted by Los Llopis. I often call my father on the spot and hand the phone to the individual. It is not uncommon for the person to shed tears when my father begins to speak in his calm and confident tone. It seems his music was for many Hispanics a lone refuge amid an otherwise turbulent and uncertain era.

After his music career, my father and mother settled in the United States to pursue an opportunity to put my father's chemical engineering studies to work. Through his many experiences, my father learned something invaluable about good fortune— perhaps it is something immigrants like he and my mother have known for years. Good fortune is ours for the taking if only we can learn to see it.

"Opportunities are everywhere. *Pero pocos tienen ojos para ver*"—But few have eyes to see.

My father would often remind me of this when I was a boy. We came to call this skill of seeing many opportunities "circular vision." It is the ability to broaden your observations beyond what you seek and beyond the obvious details before you, and thus enlarge your field of opportunities. This skill is the first of the Four Leaves of Earning Serendipity, and it will elevate your career and your company.

BROADENED OBSERVATION

Perhaps a story from history will further illustrate this skill.

In 1941, a Swiss man and his dog went hunting in the foothills of the Alps. Upon his return home, the man found dozens of burrs clinging to his pants. For most, this would be a bothersome observation; to him, it was an exercise in curiosity. An electrical engineer by trade, the man's keen eyes sensed something beyond the obvious. He pulled a burr from the leg of his pants and viewed the small item under a microscope. What he observed would change his fortune forever.

Tiny hook-like arms protruded from all over the burr's round body. The man immediately knew it was these tiny arms that allowed the burrs to cling to the fabric loops of his pants. An opportunity then came into focus. If he could re-create the hook-like design of the burr's arms and pair it with a strip of loop-filled cloth, he could create a new fastener. George de Mestral would eventually name this fastener Velcro and go on to cultivate his obscure observation into a multimillion-dollar company.

To say de Mestral met with luck on the hunting trail that day is shortsighted. His serendipity was surely earned, and it began with broadened observation: the practice of seeing with circular vision.

Observation for Opportunity

You've heard it said that there is more than meets the eye, and most accept this notion blindly and without cause for action. In truth, there is always more than meets the eye. Every circumstance, every conversation, every relationship contains the potential for numerous observations beyond the obvious and, consequently, for numerous opportunities. That which meets your eye determines the opportunities available to you. And more than any other factor, the opportunities you see determine your potential for success.

Those able to see more than the obvious possess a skill that will both protect them from misfortune and point them toward good fortune. This takes place when one sees not only straight ahead but also (1) around, (2) beneath, and (3) beyond what is before him or her. Applying circular vision in two primary environments will protect and expand the best opportunities before you. These environments are

1. Conversations

2. Adverse Circumstances

I will illustrate how circular vision takes place in each environment.

ENVIRONMENT 1: CONVERSATIONS

The best way to illustrate the skill of circular vision in conversations is in the context of a meeting. While most conversations take place outside the walls of a meeting room, I've found that when one learns the skill in a multiple-conversation setting, it then becomes simpler for the individual to apply it in a less-complex environment.

To apply circular vision in this manner, you must always remember that the meeting is not the point of the meeting. With this mind-set, your eyes will begin to observe more than the colors on a chart and the steps on an agenda. These things are plain to anyone, and observation of them rarely initiates new opportunity. Circular vision allows you to see more and thus enlarges the field of opportunity arising from the meeting.

See *Around* the Obvious in Conversations

Look around the obvious details of the meeting to the people and the social dynamics that exist in the room. Look around the job titles and designated seating positions to spot the real leader. Perhaps an executive is heading up the meeting but another wields the most influence when discussions begin. Observe who owns the respect of the room. Who is trying too hard? Who is posing? Who is apathetic?

Take good mental notes because the social dynamics of the room will tell you much about whom you ought to align yourself with and whom you should not. If you are in a position of leadership, noting the social dynamics in the room will tell you who can take the department, the company, or the venture at hand to new heights.

Whether or not you are in a position of leadership, your fortune is inextricably linked to your collaborations with other people. You must therefore know who will help and who will hinder your propensity to succeed. There are four primary characters you must always identify:

1. The Leader
2. The Loafer
3. The Leech
4. The Lifter

The Leader

The Leader is the one who holds sway in the room. Leadership expert John Maxwell once asserted that the observant person can pinpoint the true leader in a meeting in less than five minutes. The Leader is not always, and perhaps rarely, the one with the most words. He or she is the one the people respect, and the one who holds the most influence. When the Leader speaks, the majority listens. The others in the room offer support to the real leader through nonverbal cues such as smiling, nodding, direct eye contact, and adjusting their seating position to face the Leader. Oftentimes, when the positional leader (who is not the real leader) is speaking, others in the room are fidgety, they stare at the table or off in the distance, or they carry on nonverbal conversations with coworkers.

I do not suggest here that most positional leaders are not the real leaders. It is my experience, however, that it is best to not assume position equals influence but instead to enter a meeting with a clean slate and make your observations from an unobstructed view. Remember that nearly every great CEO was once a typical employee sitting in meetings with bosses and coworkers. And nearly every great entrepreneur who set out on his own was in the beginning an unpositioned leader with untapped potential. To align yourself with such people is not only a wise strategy, it opens the door to opportunities you could not access on your own. Will not such leaders recruit those closest to them, those they trust, to join in their ventures? It has always been so, and you would do well to position yourself in their camp.

The advantages of spotting the Leader in a meeting are fairly obvious. This is the person with whom you ought to align yourself more than any other individual. Not only will you learn from the Leader, you will quicken your experience and you will position yourself to climb as the Leader climbs. I have seen this time and again in my corporate experience. As the Leader moves up, so does the Leader's inner circle. As the Leader succeeds, so do his closest supporters. Put simply, those aligned with the real leaders in any organization will receive portions of good fortune unavailable to the rest. Some four thousand years ago, ancient Israel's third monarch, the wise King Solomon, said it this way: "He that walketh with wise men shall be wise."[1]

We speak of one being guilty by association, but the opposite is equally true: one is also successful by association.

The Loafer

The Loafer is, conversely, one you must avoid. He is the one to whom good fortune remains unseen. To be aligned with him is to blind yourself to various opportunities and stunt your potential. To observe the Loafer in a meeting is straightforward. He is the one who is late, unprepared, and uninterested. While meetings can certainly achieve high levels of boredom, the Loafer takes apathy to a new level, primarily evidenced by a lack of involvement. The Loafer will rarely make his idle stance obvious in the presence of a superior (and therefore rarely in meetings in which one is present), but his nonverbal cues invariably give him away: roaming eyes, slouched posture, lack of note-taking tools, and a static seating position regardless of who is speaking.

Concerning the Loafer, the ancient Roman philosopher Horace offered proper advice: "That destructive siren, Sloth, is ever to be avoided." To identify and then avoid close association with the Loafer is to avoid misfortune. This in itself is a measure of good fortune. The Loafer lacks the sight to see his own opportunities and therefore can only hinder the sight of yours.

The Leech

The other character in your workplace with whom you should avoid close association is the one who is unwilling to participate in solutions and innovations but is over-willing to eat from the harvest of success. The Leech is more difficult to spot than the other characters because he is typically agreeable and excitable. He is easy to be around and easier to keep around. But beneath the surface, he makes no real sacrifice to achieve success and offers no extraordinary value to coworkers or the venture as a whole. Perhaps he fills an empty seat, but he fills it with little more than hot air. We often call the Leeches in our organizations "yes-men" and "yes-women." They arrive on time and do what they're told, but little else.

To spot the Leech in a meeting you must understand the basic rule by which he lives and breathes: Be safe. To follow this rule, the Leech will always side with the majority, will never question the position of authority, and will almost never take a stance of his own. While he gives the appearance of involvement, he rarely poses a legitimate new thought or new course of action. He will, in fact, offer his "new" ideas by rephrasing one already posed (at times in an attempt to claim the idea as his own). He will consistently take the safest position, giving little thought to what is right or wise or innovative. His goal is to remain in the good graces of important people—to remain secure—in order to keep his job. The danger in a close association with him is that he will always see what you see, and nothing else. He has no sight of his own and therefore can do nothing but affirm or steal the opportunities before you. Such an individual will never be a catalyst of good fortune. His relationship offers you no new opportunities—no new soil into which you might sow additional seeds—and his proximity may actually pose a threat to those opportunities before you. At any point, he might steal another's opportunity in order to advance himself. He is little more than a corporate squatter and will live off your harvest and the harvest of others as long as he is allowed. There are many people more deserving and in need of a share of your harvest than he.

The Lifter

Those who do not practice the skill of circular vision will often mistake the Leech for the Lifter. You must not do so. The Lifter is no Leech. An association with her can do nothing but expand the field before you. She is capable of offering value through supporting action and self-initiated action. The Lifter is not fearful of questioning the status quo or the person of authority when necessary. She does so in a tactful but clear fashion when the best solution or strategy is in danger of being lost.

In essence, the Lifter is a Leader in the making. She is not typically in a position of authority, but she makes the most of the resources given her and is clearly interested in personal and professional improvement. In a meeting room, she is actively involved. Her nonverbal cues give clear support to her passion and full engagement. She takes notes, faces each speaker, and listens actively. Her words, while not always well spoken, clearly indicate her motive to work toward the best conclusion. She is perhaps prone to argument to stand up for what she believes, but her unilateral humility makes her forgivable.

To maintain association with the Lifter has twofold value: one, she is a steady ally in the pursuit of good fortune because she will always offer an honest opinion and at times a new insight; and two, her ability to maximize her resources makes her an expander of opportunity. While she may not be naturally creative, her commitment to excellence will open doors through dedication and persistence. Sowing a seed into a relationship with her is an investment in a future harvest. The Lifter will eventually blossom into a Leader with a larger field of opportunities. If you have cultivated your relationship with her along the way, you will share in her harvest.

Seeing *Beneath* the Obvious in Conversations

Once you develop the skill to see *around* the obvious details of conversations, you will be able to quickly see *beneath* these same conversations. When I speak of seeing beneath conversations, I am referring to the political environment that exists. Most do not possess the eyes to observe the underlying motives, power plays, and signs, and such people are prone to be blindsided by misfortune. I must tell you I was once on the wrong side of the equation and this is why I understand.

I had developed and launched a gourmet-food product line that was to be sold in Costco, Albertsons, Kroger, Safeway, and Big Lots stores across the nation. Millions of dollars were in the pipeline, and it appeared that my harvest of good fortune would soon grow exponentially. At this time I met a man who would become my partner in the licensing of the products. I trusted him somewhat blindly and now, looking back, can see the political signs beneath our conversations that pointed to the unfortunate outcome.

It seemed each time we spoke about the details of the venture, he referred to questions or concerns his business partner had brought to his attention. I addressed these matters honestly and tactfully, seeing the concerns in only an obvious manner. I considered them merely part of due diligence even though the partner was not formally involved. The unfortunate truth beneath the surface was that the man's partner, who I later found out was his wife, held his power card, and I posed a threat to her. My licensing partner was only a pawn, and in the end his wife talked him into breaching our contract. I was blindsided. His decision to disregard our agreement landed us in arbitration and eventually withered all profits from a once-promising harvest.

The imminent outcome is obvious to me now, but at the time my excitement to reap a large harvest prohibited me from seeing the politics beneath the surface. They clearly indicated the man wasn't the right partner. While he was pleasant, he was neither a

Leader nor a Lifter, and my involvement with him caused me misfortune I could have avoided.

To avoid a similar outcome, you must learn to spot the signs of damaging political undercurrents beneath your workplace conversations. Unnoticed, they are weeds that choke seeds of good fortune. Left to thrive, these political weeds will destroy an abundant crop of opportunity.

There are three primary political weeds that root themselves beneath the surface of workplace conversations. While many other weeds can exist, you must learn to spot and uproot these three, above all others, in order to maintain a momentum of good fortune.

1. Distrust. Trust is easy to spot; its antithesis is not. Distrust will not show itself in obvious fashion because distrust knows it is not welcome. It will hide and only become visible to those with the skill to see beneath the obvious. The ability to spot the weed of distrust is not simple, but all weeds of this nature look alike.

Spot distrust once and it becomes easier to spot again.

Let us go again to the meeting room to provide an illustration. And let us suppose you are in a meeting with both executives and coworkers to discuss the future of the company. If you have eyes like most, you will only see what is expected: positional leaders offering evidence of a good harvest to come. Is this not what such people are expected to do? Is this not what workers have become accustomed to hear? It is, but what is expected often keeps us from seeing what is true.

When distrust is present beneath the surface of an organization, executives will withhold full disclosure in meetings where employees are present. This does not mean a disaster is imminent, but it does indicate an unstable foundation that is unable to sustain a momentum of good fortune. Many make the mistake of assuming it is the leadership's duty to be optimistic—that it is perhaps in the company's best interest to paint an optimistic picture in order to keep employees motivated. It is not so. When the Leader trusts her people and, perhaps most important, trusts her own ability to lead, she will paint an accurate picture of the company's present crop and future harvest knowing this is the soundest path to success.

Trust must exist between an organization and its people for good fortune to be earned and then sustained. Every company must face the challenges of a marketplace full of unpredictable variables—as a farmer must face the challenges of unpredictable weather. This will surely mean that some harvests will be better than others for reasons a company cannot always control. But for an organization to continue in a tradition of success—despite the effect of unpredictable variables—trust must be its soil. It is therefore significant to observe the ground in which your company's roots are planted.

Look beneath the details of your next company meeting. What political undercurrents exist? Is the leader merely making the expected power play, puffing himself up and blowing a smoke screen to cover up the truth? Can the leaders be trusted and do they trust the workers? Are the discussion topics in the meeting subjective, vague, and seasoned with optimism? Or are they objective and supported by the obvious observations in your workplace?

If you see that distrust exists beneath the surface of your organization, you must understand the implications and then act accordingly to preserve a momentum of good fortune. This again goes back to the significance of association. You can fail or succeed merely through the organization with which you choose to associate. If the company for which you work is planted in bad soil, not only will it struggle to bloom, so too will you. The longer you maintain your association, the smaller your field of opportunities will shrink. On the other hand, when you associate yourself with an organization planted in the soil of trust, your opportunities will increase in measure with the organization's growth.

2. Indifference. Indifference is perhaps the simplest of the political weeds to spot. In conversation, indifference shows itself in an inability to make a clear statement, offer a definitive opinion, or provide tangible involvement. I have observed many people who do not realize they are displaying such signs, but their ignorance does not remove their greater propensity for misfortune than good fortune.

An indifferent leader will lead you and your company no closer to good fortune than one who drops one quarter in each of three different slot machines. The odds of success are random and unpredictable at best. To attempt to sustain a momentum of good fortune under her leadership is equally unpredictable.

An indifferent coworker or business partner will make it difficult for you to grow the best opportunities when they arise. He has neither the eyes to see good fortune nor the skills to seize and sustain its growth. These deficiencies will damage the soil of your field of opportunities. You must remove yourself from association with him in order to be unaffected by his misfortune and keep yourself unencumbered to see, sow, grow, and share the good fortune all around you.

3. Lack of integrity. This political weed is a harvest killer. When lack of integrity is evident beneath the surface of conversations, it is a sign of imminent disaster. It is easy to mistake lack of integrity for indifference. Perhaps this is because we always lean toward giving others the benefit of the doubt. We would prefer to ascribe lighter character flaws to people if we must ascribe any—especially to those we work with on a regular basis. This is a good quality present in most human beings. However, we cannot in the name of good faith blind ourselves to what is imminently damaging to us.

When lack of integrity is spotted, it must not be ignored. It shows itself most often in inconsistency. By this I do not merely mean a person not doing what she said she would do. This is an obvious observation. In conversations, lack of integrity shows itself in a subtler manner—through the slight changing of opinions and exchanging of loyalty.

Lack of conversational integrity often gives the appearance of affability. The saleswoman's manager offers an opinion on the slowing of sales in the first quarter. The saleswoman nods, and along with the rest of the room, she turns to see the COO's response. He disagrees and as he does, the saleswoman affirms his position through subtle nods, note taking, and direct eye contact. Perhaps you are tempted to see this as a benign episode of kissing his backside. It is more than this. When a person—be she your leader, coworker, or partner—pays often into the strategy of making the most important person happy, she cannot be trusted to do what she says. It is impossible to uphold such an agenda and simultaneously sustain good fortune. Some opportunities go against the grain. You must therefore make certain to avoid close associations with this person to keep your field of opportunity wide and fertile.

Seeing *Beyond* the Obvious in Conversations

Enacting this element of circular vision requires an ability to detach from the emotional effects of conversations. There are two sides to this skill, and you must embody both to ensure that you maintain sight of your best opportunities.

1. See beyond the negative effects. I am referring to those personal or professional verbal jabs directed at you or those with whom you are aligned. You must see beyond them or they will blind you to other opportunities before you. Anger, hate, and disappointment are the more-common effects of such occurrences, but these emotions force one to keep an eye open for vindication and justice. Spending time on this fruitless search leaves an individual with only one eye to see the better opportunities before him. This not only hinders your ability to sustain good fortune; with half your vision focused on a fruitless seed, it also leaves one side of you unprotected from misfortune.

Seeing beyond negative effects of conversations also refers to seeing beyond the character flaws that you have spotted in others. While you must, as we learned earlier, use such observations to determine who will help or hinder your momentum of good fortune, if you do not learn from and then leave these observations behind, they will turn you arrogant, pious, and judgmental. This will eventually blind you to maturity in those with whom you work.

After the misfortune with my licensing partner and his wife, I faced the difficult prospect of seeing beyond my anger and great disappointment with them. I was also angry at myself for having allowed the debacle to happen. "How could I have been so blind?" I asked myself. How could I have not seen it coming? How could people act in such a dishonest and disrespectful manner?

When I saw the blindness my anger and disappointment were causing, I sought help. I was having difficulty letting go. Near my home in Southern California is the large Saddleback Church, pastored by the author Rick Warren. I made an appointment to speak with a counselor on staff there, and her kind wisdom reminded me of something my father once told me. He said,

> "A man's fortune is never won or lost in one instant. *Es siempre una culminación"*—It is always a culmination.

My counselor and my father are correct. By retaining my anger and disappointment, I had ignorantly placed my fortune in the pinch of one instant. It did not belong there—and would not grow there—on that tiny divot of land. This wisdom allowed me to step back from the microscope through which I'd been peering and once again see that before me was not only a still-plentiful harvest of many blooming seeds but also much more land yet to be harvested.

Perhaps you have been offended by a workplace conversation or angered by a business interaction. While your emotion may be justified and vindication may seem the only right conclusion, you must learn to see beyond the effects of such conversations. Who knows whether the offender will by remorseful or duly penalized for what she has done? Her fortune is not for you to decide. You can control it no more than the wind or the waves. You must control only what you can.

You must keep your fortune in your own hands.

2. See beyond the positive effects. Perhaps this statement confuses you. I understand your confusion, but I have found that seeing beyond the positive effects of conversations is, for most, more significant than seeing beyond the negative. I will explain.

We are by nature positive people. We want to believe in what is good and true. We lean toward hope. We therefore find it difficult to temper our excitement and subsequent actions following a favorable conversation in the workplace.

A marketing rep receives news from the CMO that he is the front-runner for the director position opening up in a couple of weeks. It is wonderful news and certainly an indication of potential good fortune—the fruit of an opportunity he cultivated well. The man leaves the morning meeting on a high and two hours later celebrates at lunch with friends. That night he shares the great news with his wife and other family members, all of whom affirm he is quite deserving of such good fortune. That weekend, he treats his wife to a nice dinner and then urges her to go on a shopping spree the following morning. She deserves it, he tells her; and they will soon have plenty more money.

Perhaps he is right. Perhaps he is not. The problem is that he has not yet won the position. While he's received a good word, much can happen in a couple of weeks. Minds change. New prospects arise. Job openings close. I have seen this occur more times than can be counted. And if one like the marketing rep cannot immediately see beyond the instant gratification of good news, he is in danger of a double misfortune: He does not win the position and he must also deal with the frustration, embarrassment, and perhaps debt that result from his myopic, inconclusive reaction.

The one who sustains a momentum of good fortune understands that the positive effects of workplace conversations can encourage and inspire us but should never be the sole catalyst to action. Perhaps it is in the workplace that the maxim "actions speak louder than words" is most applicable. This is equally true of flattery and praise from bosses and coworkers. Perhaps the coworker who has been lauding your great work ethic is about to campaign for you to pick up his slack. Perhaps the boss who has been singing your praises is going to ask for an introduction to a lucrative prospect your family knows.

I tell you these things not to encourage your distrust of those with whom you work; I tell you these things so that you will keep your legitimate opportunities in sight and not attempt to grow a seed that is not yet sown.

If a boss has given you a good word—perhaps an indication of a potential upgrade to your position—don't speak of it widely. You may allow it to raise hopes, but do not yet act upon it in a personal or professional manner. Let only the tangible conclusions of your positive conversations lead your steps. Who can know if a hopeful supposition will come to fruition? Only firm actions will make it so.

If a coworker gives you regular praise, receive it with gratitude and then allow your circular vision to confirm any subsequent opportunities. Is this person a Leader or a Lifter? If so, perhaps the soil is being prepared for a deeper relationship.

You must remember that business culture is a melting pot of egos and agendas. Many words spoken with positive overtones carry negative tendencies. Many words spoken with cooperative overtones carry selfish tendencies. To act on overtones alone is to align with potential misfortune. You must learn to look beyond these initial effects.

I do not mean to put a damper on conversations that ought to excite us and elevate our hope. For certain, many positive conversations are authentic and point to good fortune that does bloom. And one can certainly learn to discern which are authentic by knowing from which of the four characters they originated. However, I tell you it is best to always temper your initial reaction to positive conversations and reserve your emotions and resources for tangible opportunities. Such opportunities are primarily a result of a growing relationship with perpetual signs of continued growth.

Where the positive and negative effects of conversation are concerned, you must learn to see beyond the instant emotion and allow broader observation to confirm tangible opportunities before you. Have her words consistently been backed by action? Are the manager's suppositions typically empty words—merely corporate hype? Whose words are trustworthy? Whose are not? To continue earning good fortune, you must back away from instant dejection and instant gratification and widen both eyes to the field of tangible opportunities before you.

ENVIRONMENT 2: ADVERSE CIRCUMSTANCES

To apply the skill of circular vision in the second environment is more than embodying the act of turning a negative to a positive. Seeing the obscure opportunities in adverse circumstances must certainly begin with an optimistic perspective, but the one who keeps good fortune on her side despite adversity must do more than remain positive that "this too shall pass."

I must admit that I have experienced more adversity as an entrepreneur than as a corporate employee, and I have thus come to trust circular vision in this arena all the more. I believe it is the only way to avoid losing one's momentum of good fortune.

There is more than one cause of adversity, but I do not speak here of the adversity that comes as a result of laziness, dishonesty, or illegal activity. The one to whom adversity comes as a result of these sources is deserving of his misfortune. His only path to fortune is to turn from his ways.

The adversity of which I speak comes unpredictably, like a sudden wind or an overnight frost in summer. While we might prepare by looking to history or listening to the corporate meteorologists, it is simple fact that some adverse circumstances just come unannounced and unexplained; we can do nothing but react. Yet how we react is everything. It ultimately determines whether one sustains or surrenders a momentum of good fortune.

Risk and Adversity

As an entrepreneur, I have learned one thing above all about adverse circumstances. It is a certainty that those who venture more risk more adversity. The way to good fortune is often peppered with risk. Yet this is no reason to shrink from opportunity. Risk is always the gap between opportunity and success.

You must therefore make risk your friend. She is at times fickle,
but without her the greatest seeds will not grow.

A wise farmer sows many seeds knowing full well his work will not guarantee that every seed will grow into full bloom. He accepts that there are certain circumstances he cannot completely control, and he thus knows some of his seeds will inevitably not grow. Yet he sows as many seeds as the field before him will hold. While he always finds that the bulk of his land is well suited for growth, the wise farmer understands that the more he plants, the more he might reap. He always bears in mind that he can never fully know the mind of the sky and soil.

It is in this way—sowing as many seeds as his land will hold— the wise farmer comes to know that growth is more likely than death, and gain more likely than loss. We will learn much from this wise man in the chapters to come, but we must first understand how his wisdom prepares us to see more than the obvious opportunities in adverse circumstances.

To put this in terms we can understand in the business world, the wise farmer teaches us that the most significant lesson of adversity is not that it is merely part of life but, rather, that it is increasingly irrelevant when occurring amid a growing host of successes.

To the fortunate man, a misfortune is barely noticeable.
To the unfortunate man, a misfortune is doubly intense.

Here you must understand something about sustaining good fortune: It is not embodied by merely ducking misfortune. While there is much adversity to be avoided in the workplace, the ability to sustain a momentum of good fortune is ultimately a matter of force: The boulder does not stop the river whose current is large and fast, yet it dams the trickling stream.

Many in the business world see only the boulders before them, and it gives them cause to lament, linger, and lose hope. They lose momentum and are vulnerable to more misfortune. In essence, those who cannot create a momentum of good fortune are slave to the strongest current around them. If it is misfortune, this too will be their lot.

Others, the rare few who keep good fortune on their side, learn to look around, beneath, and beyond the boulders for the less-obvious-but-always-present opportunities to be seized. In this way they sustain a momentum of good fortune despite adverse circumstances.

Seeing *Around* the Obvious in Adverse Circumstances

My father often said,

> "Adversity is very big when it is all you can see. But it is very small when in the presence of all else that surrounds you."

The key to seeing around adverse circumstances is a matter of focus. Zoom in on it and you will see no opportunity. Zoom out and see it in the context of all else that surrounds you, and many opportunities will come into view.

The best opportunities that arise from adverse circumstances always surround the equity present in the experience. This equity is what most see only in hindsight, many months or years after the events. Most eyes are frozen on the insecurities of adversity. However, one must not allow this insecurity to keep her eyes from looking around at the equity of the experience—what the adverse circumstance is revealing about herself and the field before her.

The richest equity of an experience is grounded in the immediate opportunity to take inventory of your current assets—your relationships, your skills, and your leverage.

It has been said that adversity makes or breaks you,
but adversity primarily reveals *you.*

In the midst of adverse circumstances, the one who creates and sustains good fortune is the one who allows adversity to clarify reality. In this way, adverse circumstances are like a new lens. Perhaps they clarify something about ourselves we've overvalued. Or perhaps they clarify a strength we've never employed.

An IT manager receives notice that his company is downsizing. In thirty days' time, his position will be downgraded to part-time. He is thirty-one, married, and the father of two young children. It is not feasible that his family can live on only half of his current salary. The man knows he must find another option and has two ways of going about it.

Most would panic in this situation and take the first opportunity in sight. This is often the equivalent of sowing a seed that will not grow. While finances will at times dictate how one must pursue a new opportunity, finances cannot be the sole criterion for action. I have found that if only one would have opened his eyes before leaping at the first dollar in sight, he'd have seen a host of more-fruitful opportunities before him. In this age, open communication and collaboration can quickly expand your field of opportunity.

Instead of panicking, the IT manager spends an hour that evening listing the people with whom he has a strong rapport: friends, family, close colleagues, and longtime clients. He composes separate e-mails to each of the four groups, briefly explaining the news he has received and then asking one simple question: What opportunities do you see before me?

This action accomplishes two things:

1. Compiles the observations of those who know him best, which culminates in a list of his most visible skills—some of which he'd never seen.

2. Involves those who know him best in the search for opportunities. Those closest to the man will want him to succeed.

The man has immediately broadened his observation by focusing many eyes on his situation. These advocate eyes see for him.

The manager has also expanded his field of opportunity by peering onto the fields of those who want his success. The fields of those closest to him will bring forth opportunities he might never have seen. They will do so all the more when the fields are those of Leaders and Lifters with growing harvests of their own.

While you are no doubt tempted to believe this example is oversimplified, this is the full view most never see around them in the midst of an adverse circumstance. This example is also based on an actual experience that resulted in the manager launching an IT services firm of his own, which catered to three of his former company's competitors. Nearly one-third of his staff also joined him in the opportunity.

It is always simplest and most common for one to continue in the comfort of the path he is on. It takes circular vision for one to continue seeing and seizing better opportunities. Yet I assure you, better opportunities are always present—often more so in the midst of adverse circumstances. Perhaps this is why my father often asserted,

"The point, my son, is never the job. *Es la oportunidad dentro del trabajo*"—It is the opportunity within the job.

There is one thing every fortunate person understands that the common man does not: Adversity is more valuable than well-being if it creates a better opportunity. The fortunate one continually ensures this is so. Adversity then becomes for him a tool for keeping good fortune on his side.

Seeing *Beneath* the Obvious in Adverse Circumstances

I have said that opportunity is the mother of success, and it is therefore the creation of new opportunity that compounds success more than any activity. The fortunate man creates more opportunity by seeing beneath adversity than the common man creates by seeing only the obvious options before him. Adversity, you see, is a more-efficient teacher than knowledge. It offers us tools we don't yet know we lack.

Is this not why those who have overcome adversity can claim they would not trade the experience for the world? Do some not confess they are far better for it . . . and have gained more from it than if the circumstance had not occurred? There is common wisdom in these claims. And still many quickly forget this wisdom in the midst of an adverse circumstance.

The one who sustains good fortune does not forget.

Look beneath adverse circumstances and you will find tools forged ahead of their time—tools you might otherwise take years to acquire. These are stronger and more dependable than the tools of common education. They prepare the soil of your field to receive good-fortune seeds of which you were not previously aware, and they also protect your field from sudden disaster.

LESSONS FROM THE UNDERGROUND

In the seventeenth century, the wise farmer learned he must continually sow new and different seeds in his field in order to maximize the soil and maintain the fortune of a good harvest. However, this "crop rotation," as it came to be called, was not always a regular practice.

Why go through the trouble of sowing new seeds in a soil already proven to reap a particular harvest? It once seemed more sensible to prepare a soil for one particular crop and then cultivate the same trustworthy harvest each year. The inherent (for centuries unaddressed) problem with this strategy is that it ultimately left the farmer vulnerable to nature's whims without alternate options for success. The lesson many early farmers learned the hard way was that if the nitrogen beneath the surface of their soil was not moderated, an entire crop was at the mercy of a number of great misfortunes: insects above the surface, fungal pests beneath the surface, and ultimately, fallow ground. A grand harvest one year could become a great loss in the next year. The early farmer could labor much at his crop, but ultimately his success relied heavily upon the hope that the winds of fate would treat his seeds favorably. Are not many careers built on the same foundation?

To moderate such misfortune, early Dutch farmers made two significant discoveries beneath the surface of the common farmer's adversity. The lessons they learned embody the best opportunities available to those skilled at seeing beneath adverse circumstances.

Lesson 1: Adversity is opportunity for positive change.

First, the Dutch farmers found that when a new crop replaced the former year's crop, over the course of a four-year rotation, the soil maintained a proper balance of nutrients. Specifically, they learned that this regular changing of crops moderated the soil's nitrogen content and kept the fields fertile, ensuring a continued harvest year after year. It also prevented the build-up of insect and fungal pests who tended to like one crop and not another. This illustrates for us an important lesson about the value of regular change.

While adverse circumstances are for the common man merely an obstacle to overcome, they are for those who earn good fortune an opportunity to make positive change. This tool of change is more powerful than constancy if it is wielded properly. It is not enough to see beneath adverse circumstances and merely acknowledge the opportunity to change. My father explained to me,

"Without strategy, *el cambio es sólo sustitución*"—change is only substitution.

To ensure that change propels you forward and plants additional seeds of good fortune, you must marry the opportunity for change with your current inventory of skills, relationships, and leverage. If you recall, this inventory is the first opportunity adverse circumstances offer you.

The IT manager had eyes enough to see that his looming salary cut was no thing to be taken lightly. Change was clearly forthcoming. Yet up to this point, he'd made no uncommon observation that would create and sustain good fortune. But he accomplished this when he looked deep beneath the surface of the adverse circumstance instead of merely looking to spot the first available replacement income. There, underground, he found an opportunity to employ a skill he hadn't before considered—a seed of good fortune lying in wait to be sown. It remained unnoticed until a few close friends and two colleagues confirmed the manager's entrepreneurial bent. He had always been innovative, said one. A risk taker, said another. Why not start your own business? said a third. The IT manager already had a great reputation with other companies who'd admired his work for years. Why not see if he might cater to their IT needs as an independent vendor?

This he did and earned a greater fortune than if his company had never reduced his salary. Was he not then grateful for the adverse circumstance? Would he not then see the next adverse circumstance through a different lens? You must do the same. You must learn this lesson now, so the next adverse circumstance presents you with an opportunity to see and then sow greater seeds of good fortune.

Lesson 2: The right change multiplies good fortune.

What is perhaps most intriguing about the early adoption of the crop rotation strategy is that all farmers found one crop to be particularly advantageous. This particular crop thus became the staple in the four-year rotation. Appropriately, this crop was the clover.

According to recent research of historic accounts, British landowners in the eighteenth century were increasingly motivated to search for better farming methods to increase productivity and profits. The land market was active; numerous long-established landowners were being forced by debt to sell off portions of their estates, and the buyers were frequently newcomers from business backgrounds for whom ownership of land conferred the right to vote. These men regarded the running of their farms as an enterprise and sought to improve output, maximize profits, and—obviously—avoid misfortune. From 1750 onward food prices began to rise steadily with the increase in population and, after the outbreak of war with France in 1793, the disruption to food imports. High demand and thus the prospect of great fortunes encouraged farmers to look for innovative ways to raise yields.[2]

They found their best practice in the small but singularly potent clover seed—a seed with a rare quality discovered amid adverse circumstances. In combination with an agricultural technique used by the Dutch, innovative British farmers discovered that if clover seeds were sown as one of the crops in the four-year rotation, the crop would stabilize the soil through its nitrogen-fixing roots, ensuring that their fields remained fertile for future harvests. Not only that, when harvested, the clover duly fattened the farmers' cattle, whose manure further enriched the soil. The clover strategy thus proved to reap great returns in both farming and rearing stock.

Would the farmers have discovered this fortunate change in technique had not adversity originally forced them to? Perhaps they would have weeks later. Perhaps many decades later. Whichever the case, the momentous discovery was made and then applied sooner as a result of an adverse circumstance seen rightly. The circular vision of a few multiplied the good fortune of wise farmers everywhere. Had the original Dutch farmers not peered beneath the surface of their adversity, who can say when farmers would have changed their fortunes in such a significant manner.

A similar question must be asked of you and me. Would we not possess a greater momentum of good fortune had we seen beneath an adverse circumstance of our past? Perhaps you are able to look back and see those lessons now—lessons you might have learned at a much earlier time. Lessons that would perhaps have kept you from another misfortune or helped you seize a seed of opportunity you missed.

I tell you that rightly seeing adverse circumstances does as much to reverse a misfortune as it does to sustain a momentum of good fortune. Observe only the problems that are plain to see, and you will overlook the most significant opportunities before you. You must see beneath the problems to the prime seeds of good fortune. They lie there for the taking if you have eyes to see them.

Seeing *Beyond* the Obvious in Adverse Circumstances

It is true that adversity hurts. Would any fortunate person desire it? The answer is no. We are wired for the avoidance of pain and the acceptance of pleasure. So do we not then contradict our nature when we fail to see beyond adversity?

It is said that hope deferred makes the heart sick, but I tell you that recovery deferred kills the heart. In the midst of adverse circumstances we are always given the same choice:

We might look for what was lost
or
We might look for what will be found.

When one sees only what has been lost, she faces the prospect of working with impaired vision. It is not unlike trying to drive a car with dust in your eye. In the midst of all the eye rubbing, blinking, and tear dabbing, one will inevitably miss a turn, roll through a stop sign, or get lost altogether. It is very difficult, if not impossible, in such a state to see rightly the best opportunities before you. One must not allow the dust from an adverse circumstance to impair sight of what is to come.

To keep your vision clear requires an ability to see beyond the obvious details of adversity. To all, adversity is at first difficult, frustrating, and disappointing. To all, adversity first signifies that something has been lost. These are obvious observations, and to remain focused on them brings no good fortune. The question that remains is whether the future holds a greater gain than what was lost. The one with eyes full of dust will not see well enough to notice. He will spend hours squinting for sight of explanations and justifications that might remain unseen for a lifetime. On the other hand, the one who sees through the dust, beyond the obvious details of the adversity, has eyes for the good fortune yet to come.

We have spoken already of the seeds of good fortune that lie in wait for those who see *around* and *beneath* adversity. This seeing *beyond* adversity is the final application of the skill of seeing with circular vision. It is the first characteristic of a serendipiter, and it represents a critical link to employing the second of the Four Leaves of Earning Serendipity: sowing entrepreneurial seeds.

The one who has learned to see beyond adverse circumstances understands above all else that regret is a waste of time. She does not therefore allow her eyes to become lazy. Like the immigrant who comes to a new land with only ambition and hope, she knows she must look for opportunity in each moment of every day; for opportunity does not pause to be noticed. Like a sunset, it is striking for only a brief moment, and then it is gone.

SEEING WELL PREPARES YOU FOR SOWING WELL

The one who sees beyond adverse circumstances does so in an act of discipline. The application of such discipline is the skill to instinctively bounce one's eyes from the ground before him to the horizon beyond him. I have previously alluded to a term my family has used for generations: "immigrant perspective." This phrase is the embodiment of seeing beyond adverse circumstances, and it is the sum of this first skill of earning serendipity, seeing with circular vision. Perhaps it is the wise immigrant who best teaches us how to rightly see the best opportunities before us. He is a scrappy, insightful man who does not for a moment divert his eyes from the opportunities all around him.

He is always looking around, beneath, and beyond conversations to discover the Leaders and Lifters in view. He knows it is these who want the same good fortune, and it is these who are wise enough to seek it when and where it must be sought. His eyes are trained to spot the signs of distrust, indifference, and lack of integrity, as this will help him invest in the relationships with the most potential and avoid imminent interpersonal disasters. Within these relationships, he focuses on actions much more than words in order to avoid sowing seeds that will not flourish. In all, he constantly sees the best opportunities that conversations and their subsequent relationships present to him.

The wise immigrant is equally looking around, beneath, and beyond adverse circumstances. He sees around adversity and discovers the equity present in each circumstance. He does so knowing that adversity is better than harmony if it illuminates a more-accurate inventory of skills with which he can pursue better opportunities. The man also maintains eyes to see beneath adverse circumstances to spot the positive changes that will allow his good fortune to continue. He knows the path of good fortune is always changing and thus looks for the right changes that will multiply his momentum. And finally, this wise man has eyes trained to bounce from the dust of adversity to the horizon of potential. He does so knowing that regret only keeps him from future opportunities. Ultimately, his eyes protect and propel his momentum of good fortune because they set him up to sow only fruit-bearing seeds.

His next step, and yours—as a serendipiter—is to rightly sow those seeds. This is the second of the Four Leaves of Earning Serendipity.

Amazon.com

THE FIRST LEAF
Broadened Observation: *Seeing* with Circular Vision

Perhaps we might agree that many of the early dot-coms displayed to some degree the skill of seeing with circular vision. They spotted the great seeds of opportunity the Internet offered and sought to sow those seeds that would create a momentum of good fortune. Some did so in extraordinary fashion, but one company stands out, even today, above them all. It serves as a model for applying the First Leaf of Earning Serendipity in corporate fashion. This company saw beyond the obvious channels of business to what the World Wide Web might mean for global commerce. Its vision was so astute it went on to become the world's number one Internet retailer—a title it still holds today.

I am speaking of Amazon.com: the original online book retailer that now champions the realm of Internet sales. The story of how this serendipitous company began, and how it made the transition from specialty store to online super-site, is one of repeated application of the principles of the first leaf: seeing with circular vision.

The story of Amazon.com is inextricably linked to its founder, Jeff Bezos, a first-class serendipiter. A Princeton graduate with degrees in computer science and electrical engineering, Bezos immediately put his studies to work amid the mixed fortunes of Wall Street, first at the start-up Fitel, which was building computer networks to facilitate international trade, and then at D. E. Shaw, a finance firm dedicated to applying computer science to the stock market. His experiences at these two companies would sharpen his eyes to see good fortune reaching all around him.

By the time he was thirty years old, Bezos's eyes had turned toward the Internet. There he spotted an immense opportunity during a time—1994—when the Internet was predominantly used by academics and government agencies. Seeing beyond the obvious to commercial applications, Bezos saw a giant seed of good fortune in the general public's growing usage of the Internet, which was exploding at a rate of 2,300 percent per year.

He focused in further on this seed of opportunity through research. He looked first at the top twenty mail-order businesses in the United States with the intent of determining which one(s) might be made more efficient through the use of the Internet.

Books, Bezos soon discovered, were ideal. The cataloging requirements and expense made their sale impractical for mail order. On the Internet, the expense was primarily opportunity cost. A hastily arranged trip to the American Booksellers Convention in Los Angeles further convinced Bezos of the viability of selling books through the Internet. There he discovered that the industry's major players already possessed electronic lists of their products. All he needed to do was compile those lists in a central location where they could be searched and ordered by the public.

So sure was Bezos of this seed of opportunity that he gave up his lucrative New York job and its promising future. If company lore is to be believed, it was merely days later when, during the July Fourth weekend of 1994, Bezos and his wife, Mackenzie, flew to Texas, picked up a used Chevy Blazer given to them by his Cuban stepfather, Mike Bezos, and began their journey to Seattle, with Mackenzie driving while Jeff typed a business plan on his laptop. The seed of Amazon.com was being germinated even before it was sown into real soil.

It has been said that Jeff Bezos made his decision based upon what he calls the "regret minimization framework." That is, a view of looking back on life from its end to imagine the results. Though he perhaps didn't describe it as such, he was actively applying the First Leaf of Earning Serendipity. He was seeing around and beyond the obvious pathway for a well-educated, well-experienced man of his time. Today he and his company reap the perpetual harvest of that original broadened observation.

Apocryphal or not, the serendipitous birth of Amazon.com was certainly earned. It is perhaps no coincidence that the company's moniker, Amazon, is appropriately tied to the effect of seeing with circular vision. Named after the long and winding river with seem-ingly countless tendrils and tributaries, Amazon.com embodies the ever-flowing, ever-reaching nature of opportunity. Bezos envisioned, even then, a company that would manifest its namesake in scope and reach, that would carve out an ever-broadening landscape.

And the company has since its birth held to this dynamic—all from the sight of one seed. Its early operation typified what would later become the standard image of the Internet start-up. Bezos set up shop in a two-bedroom house in Bellevue, Washington. Using limited capital raised from family and friends, he designed, built, and tested the beta-version website. On July 16, 1995, after a successful month of testing, and almost exactly a year after Jeff and Mackenzie arrived in Washington, Amazon.com was finally launched to the public. The only marketing was word of mouth, and history shows us this was all it took. By the end of thirty days, Amazon.com had sold books into all fifty states and forty-five countries beyond. By November 1995, Amazon.com realized its first 100-order day and was doing more than $20,000 in sales each month.

But it was not merely this early success, fueled by an early insight into e-commerce, that gave Bezos his momentum of good fortune. He foresaw the coming wave like almost no one else. He saw that the Internet would grow quickly, that its 1994 growth of 2,300 percent was just the beginning. Perhaps most presciently, he saw the potential to transform the Internet into something that would change the way that people did business forever. He thus focused his company's energy on riding the swell as fast and as far as it would carry them.

Sensing from the beginning that books were only an entry into the online market, Bezos began to shepherd Amazon.com into other sales arenas. He did not aspire to be "Earth's biggest bookstore" but rather "Earth's biggest anything store." Again, he applied the first skill of seeing with circular vision. In 1997, he added CDs and movies, and by Christmas season 1998, Amazon.com boasted five more categories in its product line: software, electronics, video games, toys, and home improvement.

Like all serendipiters, Bezos has not seen all of his seedlings marked by extraordinary success—but the momentum of good fortune created by that original seed has been no less sustained. This is the effect of seeing one great seed of opportunity. It can elevate one's good fortune forever.

Today, Amazon.com is still the world's largest Internet retailer, handling not only its own inventory and sales but also serving as a gateway and fulfillment arm for numerous other major brands, including brick-and-mortar competitors such as Borders and Target. The future of this fortunate company is yet to be seen, but one might suspect Mr. Bezos's eyes are always roaming around and beyond the obvious circumstances before him, and they will thus continue to spot great seeds of opportunity no one else has yet seen.

Amazon.com is the story of one man who set his sights on one great seed of opportunity that would create a current of good fortune so swift it would carry on, wide and vast, for years to come. This vision consigned whole industries to obsolescence, and created one of the most recognizable brands in the world. Today, the effect of this vision continues and it serves as a clear model of the immense value of the First Leaf of Earning Serendipity. For the man who sees good fortune reaching toward him is the one whose good fortune is earned.

References

Academy of Achievement. "Jeffrey P. Bezos: Biography." www.achievement.org/autodoc/page/bez0bio-1.

Academy of Achievement. "Jeffrey P. Bezos: Interview (May 4, 2001)." www.achievement.org/autodoc/page/bez0int-1.

Edwards, Rod. "Bricks and Mortar 2.0: Amazon Fulfillment is a RW Platform and API." TechFold (blog), posted April 27, 2007. www.techfold.com/2007/04/27/bricks-and-mortar-20-amazon-fulfillment-is-a-rw-platform-and-api.

Fair, Michelle. "The History of Amazon.com." eSsortment/PageWise. http://www.essortment.com/hobbies/historyamazonc_ttas.htm.

Knowledgerush.com. "Jeff Bezos." knowledgerush.com/kr/encyclopedia/Jeff_Bezos/.

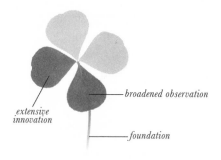

broadened observation

extensive innovation

foundation

CHAPTER 2

Extensive Innovation: *Sowing* Entrepreneurial Seeds

"The mould of a man's fortune is in his own hands."
—FRANCIS BACON

We must now move from the eyes to the hands. Those seeds of opportunity your circular vision has fortuned you to spot must now be sown into the field before you. Those who only see rightly but cannot sow rightly are the ones we call dreamers, visionaries, or idea people. They are gifted at spotting the seeds of good opportunity but lack the skill to sow those seeds into real soil. Perhaps you work with such people? Perhaps such people work for you?

They never lack ideas, and for this reason they serve good seats in a creative meeting or in a discussion centered on the company's future. But perhaps you would think twice before asking them to create the new product, design the site, close the big deal, or serve the VIP customer.

I have seen that the business world likes to categorize workers and place them on specific growth tracks. We place the one who sees well but does not sow well on the leadership track. There is good reason for this. The Leader who sees with circular vision will always set an organization up for success. Yet the question we must then ask is this: Does the organization also have those who can rightly sow the seeds of opportunity the Leader has spotted? If not, the organization will never sustain a momentum of good fortune. It will be for them as it is for most companies—success only in spurts. Up one quarter, down the next. When good vision is met with inconsistent execution, the result is an unstable fortune. The same will be so for the individual who sees with circular vision but cannot then sow entrepreneurial seeds.

SOWING AND REAPING

My father often asserted,

> "There is a critical difference between the one who sows and the one who reaps. *Usted nunca debe olvidarse esta diferencia*"—You must never forget this difference.

My father told me the following story to illustrate the difference between one who sows and one who reaps.

There once lived a wise farmer who was a man of the soil. He was a slight but strong man who labored well from the dark of morning to the fading light of day, his hands ever in the field before him. It was his great pleasure to prepare the soil in this way and then sow each seed carefully into its earthen home. Since he was a boy, the farmer had learned from experience with many crops and knew which seeds were most likely to grow in any season and any weather. He planted these seeds of greatest potential when he knew he must, and then he nourished them unto harvest.

The farmer's field was a dusty mile outside of a small Cuban town near the coast. Although the farmer preferred to spend his evenings on the veranda that overlooked his land, he and the townspeople were well acquainted because his harvests had kept them well fed for many years. When the farmer did come to town, which was not very often, the people always smiled and shook his hand. For this he was grateful, and he found much fulfillment in sharing with them.

Then one day just before the harvest, an investor came rolling down the dusty road between the small town and the farmer's land. When the farmer saw the clouds of dust approaching, he stood, wiped his hands on his shirt, and walked slowly toward the fence that bordered his field.

By the time the farmer reached him, the investor was standing on the bottom rung of the fence. As the farmer approached the investor spoke.

"Is this your land?" the man asked.

"Yes, my friend. This is my land, but its harvest belongs to all of us here."

"It is beautiful—and these crops are equally magnificent," said the investor. "You have done an amazing job here."

"Thank you," replied the farmer. "You are welcome to take something for yourself if you would like. I have just over there some very pretty tomatoes, which are ripe for eating. Please help yourself."

"Thank you," said the investor. "You're too kind. But I must tell you that I am interested in more than a few tomatoes."

"Oh, well then tell me what you'd like and we will gather it together."

"I'm afraid we wouldn't be able to gather it all ourselves," said the investor.

"What do you mean?" asked the farmer, now puzzled.

"All the way from America, I have heard about the good fortune of the soil here in the land surrounding this town. People swear there is magic beneath the surface that guarantees a great harvest every year. I heard this so often I had to travel here myself to see what the talk was all about. I arrived by boat yesterday and spent the day talking to the people of your town. Your name and this farm of yours kept coming up over and over again. Your crops, they say, are better than any around. So I have come here today to make you an offer."

"What sort of offer do you mean?" asked the farmer.

"I would like to offer you a large sum of money to buy your land—enough money to be a king in your town."

"You flatter me with your offer, friend," replied the farmer. "But my land is not for sale. This is my home, and this soil is where my hands belong."

"I agree," the investor replied. "That is why I would ask you to remain here and continue farming the land magnificently as you have for so many years."

"I don't understand," said the farmer.

"My offer is this. I will give you enough money that you would not have to worry ever again about money. You would still remain here and live and work the land each day with your skilled hands, and then each year I would take your beautiful harvest and sell the crops all over the world. I am certain many people would pay a fine price for such excellent crops."

"What about the people of my town?" asked the farmer. "Would they still have their portion of the harvest?"

"Of course they would," replied the investor. "I would negotiate with them for a fair price, and they would continue to have as much as they desire."

"I am not sure," said the farmer after a brief pause.

"Why don't you sleep," said the investor, "and I will return tomorrow. I can see that you are a man of deep thought and I have great respect for this."

"Okay," said the farmer.

"I will return tomorrow at noon," replied the investor, "after we have both had a good night's sleep. I am sure we will then both see what a great opportunity this is."

With that the investor handed the farmer a piece of paper with a large number circled on it. Then he shook his hand and said good-bye.

Ten minutes before noon on the following day, the investor's car pulled up to the front of the farmer's cottage. Again, the farmer stood, wiped his hands, and approached the fence.

"Good day," the investor called as he got out of the car.

"Good day, my friend," the farmer replied as the investor approached.

"Have you considered my great offer?" the investor asked.

"I have," replied the farmer, removing his hat. "And I have decided to turn it down with much respect and gratitude. Here, I have enough already to live as a king, and I am greatly fulfilled to simply provide for myself and the townspeople. There is no more I desire."

Greatly surprised, the investor tried to reason with the farmer for several minutes, but the farmer was not a man of fragile mind. Finally, with a frustrated shake of his head and a firm handshake, the investor tucked his briefcase under his arm and bid the farmer farewell. Before he reached his car, the investor turned back to the farmer who still stood at the fence. "What saddens me most," he began, in a bigger voice to cover the distance, "is that I will now have to become your competitor. There is much more land near this town, and its soil is the same as your soil. It too can be farmed successfully and with far greater profits. I had only hoped to include you in my great enterprise."

The farmer nodded respectfully and then returned to his soil. It was then that one of his farmhands, a young boy who had known of the previous day's exchange, asked the farmer why he hadn't taken the investor's offer. "You could have been a rich man," the boy explained, "and we would still have enjoyed our days here in this field."

The farmer reached down and took hold of the boy's wrists, turning the boy's palms upward. "Do you see this here, son?" the farmer asked, nodding toward the boy's stained hands. "The magic of which the man spoke is not in the soil as he thinks. It is here, in your hands and in mine. I did not accept the man's offer because he sought only to reap the harvest but knew nothing of sowing its seeds. Such a man's fortune cannot be trusted."

TO SEE AND NOT SOW

To sustain a momentum of good fortune, it is not enough to see opportunity in the field before you. One must also sow the seeds of opportunity into the soil of everyday activity. You must, as they say, dirty your hands.

The story of the wise farmer illustrates that the one who can see opportunity but is unknowing or unwilling to sow its seeds is afforded only an unpredictable fortune. Though he perhaps meets with success for a season, if his hands remain clean he cannot determine whether good fortune or misfortune will come next. His fortune remains out of his hands. Worse still, if the man has competitors in the same field whose hands are dirty within the soil, his fortune will truly be in their hands. If the others are skilled enough to sow rightly, they will reap the fortune of the field.

I have found that in the world of business we overvalue those who can see rightly and undervalue those who sow rightly. We tend to elevate those who see to the rare positions of leadership, and we tend to reduce those who sow to the positions of busywork. Yet the one who only sees and the one who only sows are on equal footing in the workplace. Neither can sustain a momentum of good fortune alone.

The Fate of the One Who Only Sees

While it is true that the seer is more likely to spot the best opportunities, his skill is of no use without the hands to enter and work the soil. He is not unlike a trust fund child who eats much of the harvest but has never known the hard work that made the harvest possible. Perhaps the boy becomes a man who is skilled in ideas. While his money affords him the ability to jump after his every whim, his seeds of opportunity will not grow to their potentials because he does not or cannot carry out the dirty, daily work of sowing the opportunities into real soil. This man will spend his money on one opportunity after another but only randomly succeed if his hands remain clean. This is a common character in the business world;

his potential often goes to waste. He often sees good fortune reaching out but does not possess the skill to consistently take hold of it. Unless he finds another to sow rightly for him, or learns to sow himself, he will never sustain a momentum of good fortune.

The Fate of the One Who Only Sows

The sower is no better off if sowing is his only skill. For certain, he will rarely lack a hearty income, as he knows the value of a day's work. Long labor neither surprises nor intimidates him, yet he will always work another's field if he cannot see opportunities on his own. The man who only sows will be valued for his dependability and ethic and will thus always find welcome in the workforce. But he will not be offered the seat of leadership because he lacks the eyes to spot the best opportunities. His judgment will not be impeccable. It will be said of him that he works hard but perhaps does not work smart. If he ventures beyond the field of another and attempts to work a field of his own, he is prone to sowing seeds that ought not to be sown, in fields that will not nourish. To reap a harvest, the sower must either allow another with better vision to direct his sowing or he must himself learn to see with circular vision. If he does neither, the harvest he reaps will never be his own.

SOWING MUST FOLLOW

The person or organization that strives to create and sustain a momentum of good fortune must understand that seeing great opportunities is only the beginning. This first practice must be followed by the second practice of sowing seeds into real soil. It is only in this way—through the cultivation of a well-sown field—that one can know as the wise farmer knows: that growth is more likely than death, and gain more likely than loss.

Those who regularly see with circular vision and then sow entrepreneurial seeds win half the battle. They are, we might say, on the path of success. Good fortune paints the horizon before them. Perhaps we can say they have created—earned—good fortune, and they must only learn to sustain it.

The spotting of great opportunity is a highly valued skill, but when coupled with an entrepreneurial ethic, it is a fine treasure. One can be certain there is not a business in the world that survives without both. In this way, seeing with circular vision and sowing entrepreneurial seeds are the baseline of all good fortune. Perhaps you have reason to doubt this is so.

Have we not already witnessed the fate of the leader who sees well but does not also dirty his hands? He is the one detached from his people. He is the one who trusts only his own ideas. Will not some of the people possess great vision of their own? Yes, some will even see more rightly than he. And these will grow weary if their leader will not acknowledge them. Unchanged, such a leader will never retain the most prized workers. After all, who will work for a leader who sees only for himself? The most skilled will not. And when high talent leaves a company, the leader will not last if the organization is to survive. If the organization does not rid itself of such a leader, the organization too will not last.

We have seen this played out before us. For example, the fallen giants of commerce had leaders who saw only for themselves. These leaders merely cast vision and allowed others to do the work of the soil. And then when tied to illegal activity, they claimed, "We have no knowledge of such practices," as if to say, "Blame others for the sowing. See my hands—they are clean." It is perhaps the greatest irony that leaders of large corporations today would never admit to a board of directors that they lacked knowledge of the daily sowing, yet in a legal crisis, these same leaders would quickly claim to be seers only, mere visionaries with clean hands. Such leaders cannot sustain a momentum of good fortune.

When one is eager to see opportunity but unwilling to sow its seeds, we sense something is missing. Perhaps we even sense dishonesty or an ulterior motive because he is too eager to allow the others to get dirty. There are two reasons one who only sees cannot create a momentum of good fortune:

1. Though he might be placed in a position of leadership, he will not be trusted by those he leads. He will have positional influence but not personal influence. People will follow him as a job requirement, but rarely will they follow him out of loyalty, respect, and trust. His fortune will only be as good as the people who surround him. When they leave—physically or emotionally—his fortune will change for the worse.

2. Though he knows good opportunity when he sees it, he will not do (or know how to do) the dirty work necessary to cultivate the seed. He will, as we have said, be like the grown

child of a trust fund who jumps from one venture to the next because he believes the lack of growth is the result of the wrong opportunity. The truth is that he does not understand or possess the skills to rightly sow the seed of each opportunity into fertile soil.

You have heard it said that without vision, the people perish. This much is true, but there is more you have perhaps not heard. Even if the people have vision, they will not flourish without also employing the skill to sow. I tell you there is a grand difference between surviving and thriving. Practicing only the skill of seeing opportunity will reap only survival (on the job or in the marketplace). We might say the skill is akin to making good decisions. The value is immense, and the one in possession of it will avoid many pitfalls, but one cannot thrive on it alone. It is perhaps embodied most often in the one who holds an enviable job but remains only average at employing it and never climbs higher or further.

Sowing must follow seeing if one's outstanding vision is to be of high value. When practiced together, the two skills ignite a rare momentum that closes the gap between surviving and thriving. The more an individual or company applies both, the greater the potential harvest becomes. The more opportunities that are seen and sown rightly, the higher the rate of success. This is the truth the serendipiter applies every day and to each opportunity.

SOWING ENTREPRENEURIAL
SEEDS RIGHTLY

My father used to say,

"Trust the one whose hands have held the soil; *el tiene gran potencial*"—he has great potential.

I have held this advice in every venture in which I have participated. It has protected me from misfortune as much as it has increased my good fortune. I have held key positions in several large organizations—the Gallo Wine Co., Sunkist, and the Norway Seafood Co.—and always found that those unafraid of the dirty jobs were the ones who climbed higher. They were those most adept at adjusting to the needs of the company. They were the company's most trustworthy and consistent assets. I have also found that when these were also learned at seeing rightly, they were soon to become leaders themselves.

None can dispute the vast potential of one who sees with knowing eyes and leads with eager hands. Many will follow him and many will attempt to replicate his good fortune. Only those learned in the same skills will succeed. I will now show you how this is done.

To apply the second of the Four Leaves of Earning Serendipity— sowing entrepreneurial seeds—you must always embody the two basic ingredients of proper sowing. This is as true for the individual sowing in the field of his career as the organization sowing in the field of the marketplace. The one who does not heed the two ingredients of proper sowing is like the novice farmer who believes that all seeds grow with mere dirt and water. Is this not oversimplification?

The wise, experienced farmer has learned that the depth of soil and amount of water are also critical. He also knows that the season in which a seed is sown is of utmost importance. An ill-timed sowing is no different from tossing seed onto an asphalt road—nothing more than wasted opportunity.

This novice farmer, if he is to ever earn a harvest, must learn what is foundational to successful sowing. So too must the one who will continually earn a harvest of good fortune in his company or career.

THE TWO INGREDIENTS OF SUCCESSFUL SOWING
Ingredient #1: Proper Timing

The wise farmer sows seeds in season to give each its best chance to grow. He knows that not every seed can be sown at the same time and therefore plants the tomato in cool soil as temperatures warm and the bean in warm soil as the temperatures cool. The novice farmer will exercise no such insight, and his learning will be only by trial and error. His harvest will not be an abundant one if he has one at all. Yet the wise farmer reaps a harvest in his first year because he sows each seed in its appropriate time.

The same is true of the one who sows his seeds of opportunity according to the proper timing. Is there not a significant difference between the one who invests in a great opportunity first and the one who waits for the majority wave to form? Will not the former one's seed reap a more-abundant crop? Yes, and it is this one who continually heeds the principle of proper timing that always sets up his seeds of opportunity to reach their potential.

You've heard it said that timing is everything, and I tell you it is most true in the pursuit of great opportunities. Do we not lament missed opportunities and closed doors? Poor timing is to blame. Do we not all know of the one that got away? Be it an opportunity in career, relationships, or finances, it is certain we all know the frustration of a great opportunity pursued in untimely fashion or missed altogether. Sluggishness is to blame. But do not as many make the opposite mistake and pursue an opportunity too soon? Their mistake is not sluggishness but impatience or lack of composure. These do not consider the new opportunity in light of the opportunities currently before them. Thus they often give up more than they gain. It is also true that there are some who do not consider timing at all. These base their decision to sow on a whim, mere emotion, or a superstition. Their mistake is ignorance—in this case, ignorance of no bliss. It is to these the ancient proverb applies: "Whoever blesses his friend early in the morning with a loud voice—his blessing is considered a curse."[3]

Yet do not all mean to increase their harvests when sowing seeds of opportunity? Yes, they do. But it is true that most do not achieve what they intend. I have found there to be three primary obstacles to sowing the seeds of an opportunity in proper timing. These are manifested in common but false beliefs that seem to permeate the mind of the common worker who cannot sustain a momentum of good fortune. To throw off these beliefs is to avoid the fate of the novice farmer who tosses more seed onto asphalt than onto fertile soil.

FALSE BELIEF:

"If the opportunity is meant to be, it will come back to me."

If you uphold this belief that you are to succeed only if it is meant to be, then you are no different from the novice farmer who stakes his harvest on the belief that the sky will bring forth rain if his crops are meant to grow. While it is true that some opportunities seem to return, this is a rare and unpredictable occasion and cannot therefore be a criterion for proper timing. Who can say whether the job will be offered again? Who can say whether the position will be filled in the moments after it was offered to you? Who can say when another company will launch the same product or service? The one who sustains a momentum of good fortune controls only what he can and thus never relies on what he cannot. One cannot control the season of an opportunity. It is said that time is of the essence, and it is only so because the seed of opportunity must be sown in season or it will not grow to its potential. The client will soon find another vendor. The position will soon be filled. The venture will find another partner. The responsibility will be assumed by another. Good fortune reaches through opportunity and it is thus ripe for only a season. Those who sustain good fortune seize it in full bloom; they understand no one can say whether it will bloom again.

FALSE BELIEF:

"If the opportunity is inconvenient, it is not right."

Believing an opportunity is not right if it is inconvenient is probably the favorite (unspoken) argument of the adult child of a trust fund. Opportunities, he tells himself, must suit my schedule. If they do not, they must be wrong. Is he not like the novice farmer who sows only when the weather is pleasant? Will not both miss the abundant harvest that comes to those willing to sow when it is not convenient? They will, and one can be certain that the best opportunities rarely suit our schedule. Is this not why we must make decisions? What determination is there to make if an opportunity is handed to us?

The nephew of the CEO receives an e-mail congratulating him on his new promotion; he is the new sales manager. Must the nephew sow a seed? I will concede that he must still make the most of the opportunity he's been given—but the first seed has been sown for him. There is no need for decisions when opportunity is convenient. We pursue the opportunity in stride. Only the fool does not. However, the difference between the one who sustains a momentum of good fortune and the one who remains controlled by fate is how one values convenience—because opportunity is no respecter of schedules. The one who consistently earns serendipity is the one who cares little for convenience. He is the one who pursues great opportunity even when it least suits his schedule, even when it frightens him. He is the one who adjusts to great opportunity rather than expecting great opportunity to adjust to him. He always does what he must. He sees great opportunity and inconveniences himself to sow seeds in it.

FALSE BELIEF:

"If I work hard, opportunities will come to me."

Perhaps it surprises you that hard work will not bring you more opportunities. I must remind you that we are not talking about productivity or work ethic—we are talking about sustaining good fortune, and the rules of good fortune do not always fit within the rules of cause and effect. For certain, hard work pays off in many ways. But I have found that hard work does not guarantee the best opportunities; it only guarantees progress. And sustaining progress is not the same as sustaining good fortune. What if the progress is wrongly directed?

The quintessential hard worker quickly climbs the corporate ladder and earns himself an executive position in seven years. For certain we will call him a fortunate man—one deserving of his promotion. But what if I told you he'd turned down two offers over the course of this seven-year stint? And of those offers, one in particular was for the same position in another company that currently paid three times what his current position earns. We might believe he had missed the greatest opportunity. While we would certainly admire his loyalty and speak of his "career success," would we not also have to wonder if he had failed to reap the most abundant harvest? Perhaps such is the case more often than we'd like to admit. While regret is certainly a waste of energy, it is the voice of opportunity missed. One must work hard but simultaneously understand that true progress is pursuing the best opportunities in succession.

It is true that hard work pays off, and I do not mean to diminish the fact—but the payoff is not always good fortune. To sustain an abundant harvest, you must possess more than an impeccable work ethic; you must also possess impeccable timing in sowing seeds into the best opportunities. My father said,

"Progress is nothing if only for the sake of progress. *El sabio salta adelante*"—The wise one leaps ahead.

Hard work is no real advantage. It is, in the world of business, merely a baseline requirement. One must work hard to remain competitive and in the realms of success. But hard workers fall on hard times every day. They fail to sustain a momentum of good fortune every year. Their misfortune can always be traced back to unsown seeds of opportunity or seeds not sown at their proper time.

How, then, does one know when the timing is right? While there are perhaps many ancillary factors and strategies that play into the decision to pursue a great opportunity, I have found that one question alone cuts through the thick idealism, fear, and false beliefs that blur the simple fact that all great opportunity is temporary and therefore must be pursued or passed. The question one must ask with every great opportunity is this: Can I handle the worst that can happen if I sow this seed? If the answer is yes—if you can handle the worst imaginable circumstance that can occur from the sowing—then now is the time to sow. You must get to sowing. If the answer is no—if the worst that can happen is all too devastating—then you must pass and give yourself more wholly to the opportunity that is already yours.

In truth, timing is no trickier than the decision the farmer faces to sow either corn or beans. The farmer's question is never actually *when* to sow, for something must always be sown in that season if a harvest is to be reaped. The question is certainly *what* to sow. In the same manner, for those who sustain a momentum of good fortune, proper timing is ultimately a question of what, not when. They are always sowing seeds and thus are always asking, "*What* seed is to be sown in this season?" When a new opportunity comes into view, the one who sustains good fortune simply determines whether the seed of new opportunity is the right answer.

Ingredient #2: Proper Depth

The wise farmer knows he must plant the celery seed shallower than the seed of his vine vegetable. The celery seed must be only one-eighth of an inch beneath the surface of the soil, while the tomato seed must be buried at a depth of at least one inch. The wise farmer also knows that some seeds must be sown merely on the surface of the soil because only light will initiate their growth. In sum, this wise man knows what each seed requires in order for it to begin reaching toward its potential. A shallow seed sown deep will reach only stunted growth. A deep seed sown shallow will rarely root enough to stand.

In the same way, the one who maintains a harvest of good fortune knows the depth to which he must invest in the opportunities before him. His options are the same as that of the wise farmer. His seeds of opportunity are to be sown (1) on the surface, (2) in shallow soil, or (3) in deep soil. I will now show you how the fortunate one determines the difference.

Seeds on the Surface: Undefined opportunity with undefined return. It is true that many opportunities come to the fortunate one in this manner. He sees them through circular vision and is intrigued, but knows he must first give definition to the seeds before going any deeper with them. In this way, the one who sustains an abundant harvest understands that many opportunities require a brief period of due diligence. These opportunities must thus be sown initially on the surface of the field before him.

While the novice will jump at the unsubstantiated promise of a big harvest, the wise man knows that an undefined seed must first come under the light of further scrutiny for its potential to be illuminated. He is first looking to answer such questions as: How much time will pass from the sowing to the reaping? Are their similar seeds that have already been harvested? How deeply were they sown? What was their return? Until these sorts of answers have been defined, he invests only on the surface. He understands that this small investment will tell whether the sowing and the reaping are commensurate. If he finds the seed of opportunity to be one that warrants a deeper sowing, he will thus invest deeper. If he finds the seed of opportunity to be one whose potential harvest does not warrant a deeper sowing, the wise man will allow the seed to remain a surface investment with an undefined return, and he will reserve his resources for deeper investments.

Seeds in Shallow Soil: Defined opportunity with undefined return. The vast majority of opportunities fall into this category. We know immediately what is required of us to sow the seed and yet do not know well what harvest will come. It is these opportunities that come to us most often, and the one who earns good fortune is prepared for them.

The top salesperson is offered the clients of the coworker who has quit. He knows immediately what will be required of him to sow this seed—the opportunity is clearly defined—but perhaps he is uncertain whether the return will be desirable. While the opportunity is flattering and is offered as a reward for his hard work, perhaps he wonders if the extra investment of time and effort will be worth the additional harvest of income. Will he lose more relational equity off the job than he gains in financial equity from the job? Will he lose a momentum of good fortune in an effort to gain a bigger harvest? It is difficult to answer such questions with certainty, and it is for this reason that most people let these opportunities pass by. This is unwise, for most great seeds of opportunity must be sown in this manner, when the harvest is not yet defined.

The wise salesperson will say yes to this opportunity, as he knows it will immediately increase his potential harvest (and as he also knows the seed of opportunity will be given to another if he does not sow it). Yet, because the seed's return is not fully defined, the wise salesperson will request that the opportunity have a trial period within which he might gain further insight into the potential return. He will thus sow the seed of defined opportunity into shallow soil by committing a predetermined period of time to it in order to define whether the increased harvest is worthy of the increased sowing. If in this period of shallow sowing the salesperson determines that the potential harvest does not warrant the investment, he will allow the opportunity to pass to another. If he determines the potential harvest is worthy of his additional sowing, he will thus invest deeper in the opportunity. Like the farmer who discovers his field is suitable for another crop, he will dirty his hands all the more to reap the greater harvest of good fortune.

Seeds in Deep Soil: Defined opportunity with defined return. Such opportunities are rare, but they must immediately be sown if one is ever to sustain a momentum of good fortune. When an opportunity and its return are clearly defined, it is only the sluggard or the fool who will not sow the seed deeply.

The manager is offered an executive position at the company headquarters in Los Angeles. The opportunity will increase his income by 20 percent and will require no more work than he currently does. The man believes in his company and is a career employee. But he is also unwise and will thus question whether the extra distance between Newport Beach and downtown LA is convenient. "I am only five minutes from work now," he will tell himself. "This will require me to wake earlier and return later. I will find it difficult to exercise so early, and my wife will not be pleased to have us eat any later. I am good at what I do, after all. This is why they are offering me the new position. So why would I change a good thing? I make enough money. Why would I throw off the nice schedule I now have? Surely, they will be just as pleased to allow me to stay put and continue doing good work." Yes, this unwise man will talk himself out of sowing the defined seed of a defined return.

Will he not soon discover that doing good work is more common than he thought? Is it not merely the basic requirement of his position? Will he not then see that his position can be filled by another, perhaps someone younger, who works just as well but in whom the company is eager to invest its training dollars? Yes, this unwise manager will soon realize that sustained convenience is no way to measure opportunity. He will learn that an ongoing harvest requires constant growth. This means one must always be sowing the seeds of great opportunity when these are before him because it is they that grow most readily—and it is they that ensure one's most abundant harvest. If one does not do this, his harvest is left to the uncontrollable elements like executive decisions, economic trends, and strength of competition. He will not know what will befall him from year to year. He is like the farmer who sows seeds without considering which seeds might require a deeper sowing; his harvest is ultimately in the hands of the wind and the weather. A strong wind would blow his seeds away. A drought would destroy his harvest.

THE FINAL INGREDIENT

In my early days of entrepreneurship, it was to my great advantage to understand the two basic ingredients—timing and depth—by which the sowing of seeds could be maximized. I had launched a gourmet vegetables brand with several products. While some insisted it was an improper use of time to study the planting of my vegetables, I disagreed. You are not a farmer, they would say. And they were correct. But my father's advice rang through their shortsightedness. I saw that if I was to sustain a momentum of good fortune in the endeavor, I must dirty my hands in the soil of the venture, both conceptually and physically. I thus learned what I have shared with you here. These lessons culminated in an understanding of the one final ingredient to all successful sowing—the one ingredient without which one cannot expect a perpetual harvest. I speak of water.

In the end, if one sees great opportunity and then sows its seed in both the right season and the right depth but does not take care to grow the seed through a strategic regimen of watering, the seed of opportunity will not reap its most abundant harvest. It is for this reason the Third Leaf of Earning Serendipity is strategic focus, or what my father calls "growing seeds of greatest potential." It is the third trait of the one we call a serendipiter.

Costco

THE SECOND LEAF
Extensive Innovation: *Sowing* Entrepreneurial Seeds

Perhaps it goes without saying that companies whose names we know are often born from a proficient application of the Second Leaf of Earning Serendipity; these companies we now know as major brands were once entrepreneurial seeds that were successfully sown. There is one company that pushes forth in my mind above all others, for it is this company with which I am personally familiar. I am speaking of Costco.

I have found that many do not know the serendipitous beginnings of this warehouse industry king. Costco was officially founded in 1983 by two veterans of retail, Jeffrey Brotman and James Sinegal, but it is certain the first seed of Costco was sown three decades earlier by a man named Sol Price.

In 1954, Price and a group of clients sowed a seed called Fed-Mart, the nation's first membership discount store, selling memberships for two dollars to government employees. Many of the basics of the now common warehouse model were hewn of this early venture. Sol Price offered deep discounts on products in stores stripped of most fancy accoutrements. By 1975, when Price sold the chain to German entrepreneur Hugo Mann, the FedMart seed had grown to forty-five stores. But this seed was to be sown again.

Mann and his executives quickly ousted Price from involvement with FedMart, and the wise Mr. Price responded by uprooting his seed and sowing it anew, making the same warehouse benefits available to the general public. Only a year later, this seedling of his original seed was cast into the soil of an airplane hangar in San Diego, California. Price Club was born as the world's first wholesale warehouse club. With the sowing of Price Club, Sol Price single-handedly blossomed a new industry and with it, a perpetual harvest of good fortune.

While it is true that Sol Price was the first sower of the warehouse club seed, we might say his protégé, James Sinegal, is the one responsible for experimenting with the original seed and sowing it in the deepest soil where the greatest growth was possible. While Price Club originally opened its doors only to business owners, memberships were soon offered to the general public to meet its great demand. Still, Sinegal remained keen on the notion that small businesses would play an important role in Costco's perpetual harvest. He thus tailored his sowing of the Costco seed to meet their needs. We might say the Costco entrepreneurial seed was sown to help other entrepreneurs sow their own.

Perhaps you will find it quite fitting that one of my first entrepreneurial endeavors found me linked to this model of second leaf proficiency. When I launched the Luna Rossa line of gourmet products as a young thirtysomething, I desired our first client to be Costco Wholesale. I sought hard to make this happen because I knew that if I could do business with Costco, I could meet the standards of almost any retail outlet in America.

I learned much of the Second Leaf of Earning Serendipity from the warehouse king. Costco demands the best from its suppliers and in this way is a strong model of sowing great entrepreneurial seeds. It insists that each of its vendors push the innovation envelope and set the bar for efficiency. From packaging, sales, and marketing to shipping and inventory management, sowing entrepreneurial seeds in Costco soil yields a more-productive and more-effective serendipiter. It is certain that this company does not permit clean hands in its fields. Those who sow in its soil must dirty their hands as the wise farmer does with his finest crops. In this way a perpetual harvest is ensured.

It is also in this way that Costco gave Luna Rossa products instant credibility. Through its unyielding insistence on the highest quality of seeds in its field, Costco has earned the trust of its members. The seeds sown in its soil are trustworthy. That my products were sold in Costco thus ensured customers and other potential partners that the products were a high-quality crop.

This same trusted reputation has also allowed Costco to cast a wide fan with its own new entrepreneurial seeds. While its core offerings of bulk consumer goods are still central to the company's success, Costco has, over the years, added consumer and business services aimed at reducing costs while improving member care. With offerings as diverse as merchant accounts, banking, and financial planning to Web development and group health plans, there is often little need today for members to venture anyplace else. These fellow sowers know that each of Costco's newly sown seeds is designed to help its members succeed in sowing their own. It is safe to say that Costco has done well to create and, in ways we will not discuss here, sustain its momentum of good fortune.

Today, Costco holds the position of fourth-largest retailer in the United States overall, after Wal-Mart, The Home Depot, and Kroger. Costco is firmly entrenched as the number one warehouse club chain in terms of sales volume even though it has approximately two hundred fewer stores than its next closest competitor, Sam's Club.

This is quite significant. Wal-Mart maintains what is arguably the mightiest supply chain and distribution network on the planet; yet, against this muscle, Costco's momentum of good fortune allows it to outperform Wal-Mart–owned Sam's Club in per-store sales and overall sales. In addition, Costco remains number one among all U.S. retailers in customer satisfaction, according to the University of Michigan's American Consumer Satisfaction Index (ACSI).

It is a safe bet that Costco's good fortune will continue as its seeds are continually sown with the trustworthy hands of extensive innovation. The result is a perpetual harvest that continues to benefit itself, its vendors, and its members. And as we have said before, when the number of those who benefit from the harvest of good-sown seeds increases, a momentum of good fortune is strong.

References

American Customer Satisfaction Index, The. "Scores by Company: Costco Wholesale Corporation." www.theacsi.org/index.php?option=com_content&task=view&id=149&Itemid=157&c=Costco+Wholesale+Corporation.

Boyle, Matthew. "Why Costo Is So Addictive." CNNMoney.com. October 25, 2006. money.cnn.com/magazines/fortune/fortune_archive/2006/10/30/8391725/index.htm.

Costco Wholesale Corporation. "Why Become a Costco Member?" www.costco.com/Browse/ProductSet.aspx?Prodid=24743&whse=BC&topnav=&browse=&lang=en-US.

FundingUniverse. "PriceCostco, Inc." www.fundinguniverse.com/company-histories/PriceCostco-Inc-Company-History.html.

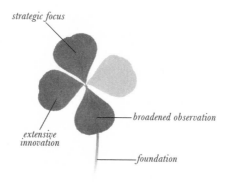

strategic focus

broadened observation

extensive innovation

foundation

CHAPTER 3

Strategic Focus: *Growing* Seeds of Greatest Potential

"Fortune favors the prepared mind."

—LOUIS PASTEUR

The wise farmer wakes early to give water to the grain and hayseed before the heat of day. He then moves to his vegetable garden to see that his irrigation is working properly, giving drink to his precious crops. Later he will sow new seeds in soil he himself has prepared, and once the seed has been placed at the proper depth, he will soak the soil thoroughly to initiate each seed's growth.

This wise man understands that water is vital from the moment the seeds are sown to the end of the growing season. While he will be certain to sow his seeds at the proper time and depth, he knows he must also be certain that his plants receive water for cell division, cell enlargement, and even for something as simple as holding themselves up. A plant without adequate water is a wilted plant. Together with light and carbon dioxide, water provides all his plants with much of the energy and nutrients necessary for maximum growth. Water is to the plant as focus is to opportunity.

The one who sustains a momentum of good fortune understands that for any seed of opportunity to flourish, it must be given a strategic measure of focus. Just as the farmer must give different amounts of water to his vegetables, his grain, and his herbs, the sustainer of good fortune must also give his seeds of opportunity different measures of focus. Each seed he has sown in the field before him will not grow to its fullest potential without proper focus. Do we not see this consequence often?

In the throes of an important department meeting, the shrewd employee spots a great opportunity for company-wide growth. He explains the idea to his manager, and the manager agrees the opportunity has great potential. "Go for it," says the manager. "You take the lead and I'll support you." Does this employee often follow through?

Is it not more common for this employee to leave the meeting and become engrossed in the details of daily work life? He has, after all, many other responsibilities he must fulfill. How can he find the time to focus on this "extra" opportunity? Will he not fail to see the opportunity through to fruition? Perhaps the employee's manager is wise and understands that her worker possesses great vision and an entrepreneurial work ethic but lacks the skill to grow new opportunities through focus. Perhaps this manager desires for the employee to see, firsthand, that the employee's skills of seeing and sowing are hindered by his inability to strategically focus.

While it is true that all face the prospect of fulfilling many responsibilities throughout a given workday, most are like the employee without a strategy for focusing on opportunities before him. Many thus merely work as smart and as hard as they can, but this is not enough preparation for focusing on the best opportunities when they arise. The majority of the workforce is made up of seers, sowers, and those who are both. The majority of the workforce is thus unable to sustain a momentum of good fortune because their seeds of opportunity do not consistently reach their greatest growth potential. The majority possesses good fortune only now and then.

A very small minority of the workforce is comprised of ones who see, sow, and grow each seed through proper focus. Their seeds of opportunity consistently reach their growth potential, and therefore they are able to sustain a momentum of good fortune. It can be the same for you, if only you will learn to consistently grow the seeds planted in the field before you. I will now show you how.

GROWTH THROUGH FOCUS

My father explained,

> "The busy man who is not successful believes opportunity equals growth. *El está como el granjero que depende de la lluvia*"—He is like the farmer who depends on the rain.

It is true that certain opportunities seen and sown will gain momentum of their own. Like seeds sown just before a season of rain, these opportunities will grow immediately and consistently. They will perhaps give the appearance of perpetual growth—of automatic potential—but this growth will rarely last to harvest. Does the wise Wall Street investor rely only on the companies in which he has purchased stock? No, he invests in opportunities he has seen to have high potential. He invests once he has dirtied his hands in due diligence. But does he then merely sit back and await his returns? No, he watches his investments carefully to know when to harvest some and when to allow others to continue growing. While rare stocks might shoot up high and fast, the wise investor understands that the only thing that ensures a perpetual harvest is not the ability to choose the rare stocks that rise fast but rather the ability to sustain a momentum of growth. This, he knows, requires a wise strategy of focus on each one of his investments.

He will thus always know which investments require his daily focus, which are nearing harvest, and which he might give less attention to, as they will grow at a steady pace. In the end, this wise investor understands that his potential for a momentum of good fortune rests in his ability to spread his focus strategically to his investments.

You must allocate your focus in the same manner to those seeds of opportunity now planted in the field before you. You must always know which seeds require the most focus, which require moderate focus, and which require the least focus. I will teach you how this is accomplished in the same manner in which I was taught. But I must first share with you two rules of proper focus, given to us by the wise farmer who waters his plants with strategy and precision.

Rule #1: Wilting Does Not Always Necessitate More Water

The opportunity that has begun to wilt may have already passed its time of harvest. At that point, no amount of water—no amount of focus—will grow it tall again. Have we not known the man who invests deeply in stock just after it has peaked? Or the one who attempts to join the venture after the profits have already begun to roll in? This man is a common one. He does not sow seeds of opportunity until he sees the fields already growing. He is merely a follower, and he is typically late. He is thus one who cannot sustain a momentum of good fortune. His timing and depth are frequently off and so his focus matters little.

Is this follower not the cousin of the one who sees and sows great opportunity but is too distracted to properly focus on it until harvest? These two are family, as neither will reap the harvest available to him—the first for love of fear and the second for lack of focus. Neither should waste his time in trying to refocus on the opportunity. Its growing season has come and gone, and now the best strategy is to focus on those still-growing opportunities in the fields before them.

The one who sustains good fortune knows that focus is required from the sowing of the seed to the reaping of harvest. If one does not properly focus during the growing season, his proper seeing,

sowing, and reaping are diminished. They could in fact be altogether meaningless.

The seeds of opportunity in your field must be sown at the
right time and depth and then consistently watered through focus.
One must not allow an opportunity to wilt due to lack of focus.

Rule #2: Always Soak the Soil Thoroughly

The wise farmer knows that a light sprinkling of water can bring
more harm to his seeds than no water at all; such activity stimu-
lates the roots to come to the surface where they are burned by the
sun's rays. Is this not like the man who merely dabbles in a seed of
opportunity he has sown, bringing its potential into the light, only
then to let it burn out? This man does not understand the principle
of focus.

The one who sustains good fortune knows that any time given
to an opportunity must be thoroughly focused on that opportunity
alone—otherwise it is not focus but a mere sprinkling of attention. For seeds to grow to potential they must have consistent measures of water over time. Their harvest is merely the culmination
of properly scheduled focus. Is it not the same with the seeds of
opportunity?

The wise farmer knows well the specific amounts of water each
seed requires and on what schedule each must receive water. You too
must determine the amount of focus each opportunity requires and
then set those amounts on the proper schedule unto harvest. Once
seeds have been seen and sown well, an abundant harvest is simply
a matter of scheduled focus. This is how one sustains perpetual

good fortune: opportunities seen well, sown well, and grown well through a cultivation of focus.

A FUNDAMENTAL HIERARCHY OF FOCUS

The wise farmer schedules his watering according to the priority of his crops in order to cultivate the best harvest. He knows that too much water will endanger the seeds' roots, and too little water will stunt his seeds' growth. You must do the same with your focus. You must schedule your focus according to the priority of the opportunities you have sown.

There are far too many individual variations—definitions of success, type of work you do, personal goals, spiritual associations, etc.—that determine the significance of each of your opportunities, and so I cannot endeavor to teach you how to properly place value on those seeds you've sown. Yet one can presume that if you have applied the Second Leaf of Earning Serendipity and have sown seeds of opportunity (1) in deep soil, (2) in shallow soil, or (3) on the surface, you must certainly believe each seed possesses a measure of potential. Would a person of good fortune knowingly pursue a worthless opportunity?

Applying the second leaf, sowing, thus assigns to your opportunities an initial hierarchy of value. You must treat this initial hierarchy as your initial template for how to grow your seeds of opportunity through focus. In other words,

1. Deep-sown seeds must receive the *most* focus.

2. Shallow-sown seeds must receive a *moderate* amount of focus.

3. Surface-sown seeds must receive a *light* amount of focus.

This is how you must begin cultivating your seeds through focus. Yet the fortunate one knows for certain that the value of opportunities can change over the course of their growth. He is therefore always aware of potential adjustments.

Perhaps one of your deep-sown seeds will grow more rapidly than the other deep-sown seeds. Will not the one who sustains good fortune give this crop more focus? He will, and for good reason. This particular crop is not only prone to reap a quicker return, it also stands to return a harvest of two to three times the value of what was initially sown. I am not merely speaking here of monetary gains. I am speaking also of the multiplication of a great seed of opportunity—when one seed sown gives birth to a host of additional seeds.

Will not certain seeds produce more than one crop in this way? The saleswoman works the soil of a top prospect. In proper time, she sows a seed deep within the soil of this relationship, and it earns her the prospect's business. If she grows this seed rightly, will she not reap more than the client's business alone? She will. In the second month of doing business, the new client is so impressed with the saleswoman's consistent focus that he refers to her the business of two colleagues. The deep-sown seed has now multiplied threefold, and the saleswoman stands to reap an even more-abundant harvest. For this reason, the one who sustains good fortune is always regulating the focus strategy to ensure the most abundant harvest.

You must remember that the one who sees a great opportunity and sows its seed can still lose the momentum of good fortune if he does not grow his seeds properly. Would not the saleswoman miss her most abundant harvest if she gave equal focus to other client relationships that were not growing as rapidly as the one with the new client? She would not reap all she could, and this will make it more difficult for her to sustain momentum. Worse still, she will be prone to remain in an unstable scenario where a weak client crop the next quarter could cancel the good fortune earned from the new client relationship. Can a salesperson survive on the harvest of only one client? Perhaps with a high-dollar product one might survive for a time. But survival is not a momentum of good fortune. What will happen when the winds of change move the main client to do business elsewhere? The unfortunate salesperson will be in peril with only a fallow field before her. Thus, it is certain that the one who sustains a momentum of good fortune thrives on a field of many growing seeds—seeds growing to their potential. In this manner, if one seed does not grow as initially thought, others still remain to create an abundant harvest.

I will remind you of the strategy I discussed, for it will make more sense to you now: It is the wise farmer who sees, sows, and grows many seeds, knowing this alone ensures that growth is more likely than death and therefore good fortune more probable than misfortune. Once his seeds are seen and sown, he maintains his propensity of good fortune through strategic focus. The serendip-iter develops this judgment with time.

A FLEXIBLE HIERARCHY OF FOCUS

My father said,

> "Change is inevitable. *El hombre afortunado ajusta rápidamente"—* The fortunate man adjusts quickly.

As I have said, it is certain that your hierarchy of focus will need to change from time to time. Perhaps a deep-sown seed will not grow and you must decrease your focus on it. Or perhaps you will in due diligence discover a surface-sown seed to have great potential, and you must therefore sow it deeper and then grow it with increased focus. The serendipiter develops this judgment with time.

Ultimately, the proper strategy is a matter of regularly prioritizing and reprioritizing your focus based on the growth of each opportunity you've sown. While you must initially give the most focus to those seeds you've sown deeply, you will inevitably need to adjust. Will a wise farmer give more focus to a new tomato garden that is merely a trial or to his field of corn, which a farmer's market has recently offered to purchase? He will give greater focus to the corn. The one who sustains a harvest of good fortune will do the same, ensuring that she is always showering greater focus on the opportunities with greatest potential.

Yes, the one who earns serendipity will at any given time be simultaneously cultivating many seeds. It is thus critical that you regularly address the specific measure of focus you give to each seed in order to grow as many as possible to harvest. The greater the perpetual harvest, the greater the momentum of good fortune. Here, now, is a breakdown of how the fortunate one invests his focus to ensure maximum momentum at all times.

Tier #1: Heavy Focus

- *Deep*-sown seeds that require *low* maintenance and promise *high* returns

WATERING SCHEDULE

1. **Focus daily.**
2. **Measure growth every two weeks.**
3. **Demote on the schedule if slow or no growth after sixty days.**

The wise farmer will ensure that his greatest investment of resources goes to those crops that require little maintenance and promise a high yield. These hardy plants represent the most sustainable and predictable portion of his harvest. To lose them is to enter into a greater measure of risk where his good fortune will be more difficult to sustain. The wise farmer knows his highest priority is to grow to maximum potential those seeds that give his harvest stability and predictability.

If you are to sustain a momentum of good fortune, you must do something similar with the opportunities you've sown. Such opportunities are those that require an uncomplicated routine of maintenance but indicate a high return on investment. The fact that seeds are deep sown does not mean they all require high maintenance. Some will require maintenance that is not labor intensive but should be given regular attention nonetheless. These opportunities that I speak of are almost always in the realm of relationships. The time, money, and effort required to grow them to harvest is minimal when compared to the value of the harvest. While these opportunities will not be as common as you like, they are more common than you know.

Do you recall our immigrant from a previous chapter? He was one who understood that of which I speak. He enters a new country with little equity, but within endless opportunities he is able to see, sow, and grow. He does not take lightly many things that the common worker would be apt to ignore. He thus will see and sow many opportunities that require little maintenance but in the end reap big rewards. The immigrant knows he can quickly elevate his fortune from the connection he forms with one individual and does so in a manner counterintuitive to most businesspeople.

What the immigrant intuitively understands is that the strongest relationships are not based on reciprocation: I will do for you only if you do for me. He knows the strongest relationships are based on generosity: I will do for you whether or not you do for me. With this understanding, the immigrant quickly forms much stronger bonds with the people he speaks to and serves. These people will remember him. They will desire to help him more readily than if he had asked them to return the favor. Some—those with whom he connected the deepest—will do legwork for him. These persons will take a personal interest in elevating his fortune. And this man, for his simple but sincere investment in another life, will receive far more in return.

Perhaps you will say that this man's investments are not as measurable in the real world. Perhaps you will be tempted to believe the immigrant is naive to the dog-eat-dog ways of business. Then I will ask you which man the wise company president will hire first: The one who has given generously to him expecting nothing in return, or the one who kissed his backside in expectation that it would earn him the position? All things otherwise equal, the wise president will hire the man who has given generously to him. It is this man that the president knows he can trust; it is this man the wise president feels more obligated to help.

If you are to sustain a momentum of good fortune, you must always be certain to water the low-maintenance opportunities that offer potentially high returns. While none can guarantee which investments will produce an abundant harvest, the fortunate one will consistently embody the relationship mantra that my father taught to me:

"Give in faith, *no en esperanza*"— not in expectation.

It is our human nature to remember those who have given freely to us. And it is these unconditional givers—those who give in faith—that will possess the greatest equity in relationships, and this for only a small investment of their focus.

It is certain you will also sow other opportunities outside of relationships that will require little maintenance and reap big returns. Perhaps a friend has requested a small investment of your money to give aid to his new business. Or perhaps you can greatly increase your business exposure into a timely, proven ad campaign. Neither of these will require high maintenance, but both have the potential for comparably high returns. It is for this simple reason they must remain your top focus. Give them your thorough focus at least once a day. Measure their growth every two weeks. Demote them on this schedule only if you have seen no growth after two months. This does not mean your strategic focus on them will not eventually reap a big return (or that the crops have wilted), but it does mean you will be wiser to refocus your efforts on tangibly growing opportunities. You must always remember that the fortunate one will give the most focus to low-maintenance, high-return opportunities.

Tier #2: Moderate Focus

- *Deep*-sown seeds that require *high* maintenance but promise *high* returns
- *Shallow*-sown seeds that require *low* maintenance

WATERING SCHEDULE

1. Focus weekly.
2. Measure growth monthly.
3. Demote on the schedule if slow or no growth after twelve weeks.

You might question whether any seed that promises a high return should be given only moderate focus. Many fall for the notion that those opportunities that require the most work will reap the greatest harvest. But this notion is not always true. Remember the green twentysomething who births Facebook while the experienced forty-somethings sweat to make ends meet? It is true that high maintenance can reap a return, but if the return is unsubstantiated—if it is based solely on hope or hype—a fortunate man can critically misallocate his focus and stunt the growth of other, more-abundant seeds.

I speak of this as a warning more than a rule. I am familiar with the harvests of high-maintenance seeds. I will concede there is little in the world of business more fulfilling than the reaping of a seed that was cultivated with much sweat and labor. But I know also that one must not allocate top-tier focus to a high-maintenance seed until its return can be verified beyond the bounds of emotion. For this reason, high-maintenance/high-return seeds must initially be watered moderately so one can measure their growth before moving them to the top tier of focus. We can be sure that certain high-maintenance/high-return seeds will end up in the top tier of focus, but I tell you that many people, in their excitement, elevate opportunities before growth is tangible. Said another way, many tend to give focus to deep-sown seeds of high maintenance that do not yet deserve such focus.

For this reason it is wisest to initially grow high-maintenance/high-return seeds in the same manner as shallow-sown/low-maintenance seeds. All such seeds are given enough focus to allow them to grow for a brief season during which you can measure them and determine whether they should be moved up or down the tiers and given an adjusted schedule.

The executive is recruited by a larger corporation than the one for which she currently works. Her call with the vice president goes extremely well, and the executive has good reason to believe in the promise of a great harvest. Does she make fewer calls each day and spend a bit less time on each report? Does she reply to the e-mails of her boss and coworkers less promptly? Does she surf the Net for new homes? Only one prone to misfortune will decrease her focus on the growing seeds before her to shower focus on a seed that has not yet grown enough to merit it.

If this person will sustain a momentum of good fortune, she will water this new seed only moderately. She will not place it in her top tier of focus until she has measured growth, for she knows that while the seed promises a great return, she must first possess tangible verification that the seed will reap an abundant harvest.

Tier #3: Light Focus

- *Shallow*-sown seeds that require *moderate* maintenance
- *Surface*-sown seeds that require *low* maintenance

WATERING SCHEDULE:

1. Focus monthly.
2. Measure growth quarterly.
3. Remove from schedule if no growth after six months.

Those seeds that ought to remain on your watering schedule but in only light measure are primarily those that require a sprinkling of due diligence. These seeds of which I speak are shallow-sown seeds and surface-sown seeds. What differentiates this level of focus from Tier #2 is your level of knowledge about the opportunity. The seeds watered in lightest measure are those opportunities and their potential returns that are still to be defined. Your strategic focus on them, at least initially, is primarily to determine the details of the opportunity itself—what it will require of you and what sort of growth season to expect. While you will be watering these seeds only once a month and measuring their growth once a quarter, they are significant crops in your field. I will explain.

The one who sustains a momentum of good fortune will always maintain a portion of his field for the studying of new seeds. This man is never done with learning. In this way, he remains teachable and open to new discoveries and greater insights. He is not unlike the wise farmer who is well versed in growing vegetables yet tills the west portion of his field for a range of new seeds each year. Will he not continue to discover additional crops that grow well in his field? Will he not continue to expand his harvest beyond that of the common farmer?

It is true that one must be careful to not give too much focus to growing undefined opportunities. But it is equally true that many an abundant harvest has been reaped from seeds initially sown shallow and watered lightly. Are not many key relationships begun in this manner?

It is human nature for us to be cautiously optimistic in professional relationships. Perhaps it is also wisest for us to begin watering opportunities in this manner. The one who consistently reaps the rich harvest of relationships is always the one unafraid to lightly water those seeds.

Two company salespeople with different regions interact on a regular basis in the confines of the workspace. Both are neither overjoyed nor disgruntled with their jobs. They work for a good paycheck and the security this offers, yet neither is climbing the career ladder. Then one coworker asks the other to lunch—she gives a light watering to the relationship. Over lunch the two discover they have much in common inside and outside their common work responsibilities. They thus begin to forge a unique bond that not only makes the work environment a more-pleasant place for each one but also raises their levels of productivity as both take steps to help the other make important connections, secure hot leads, and close important deals. Is not each worker now more influential in that workplace with a solid ally? Do not their fields of opportunity expand?

So you see that the one who sustains a momentum of good fortune does not overlook those seeds that are yet undefined. She understands that a light measure of focus might reveal certain seeds to be foundations of an abundant harvest.

THE SEEDS OF MOST CONSISTENT RETURN

The wise farmer possesses one more insight about growing the seeds of greatest potential: He knows in particular which seeds are most reliable. He thus seeks to see, sow, and grow more of these particular seeds than any other. It is true that this wise farmer will always maintain the growth of various seeds in order to sustain the stability of his yearly harvest. He must do so. Yet it is equally true that within this ever-changing variety, the wise man will always grow one particular seed more than any other: the seed of most consistent return.

The one who sustains good fortune knows well this seed, and he seeks to see, sow, and grow it more than any other. This seed of which I speak is the seed of relationship. More than any seed of opportunity, relationship seeds seen, sown, and grown well reap the most consistent harvest.

With this insight firm in your mind, it is now that I can tell you of the final leaf, the Fourth Leaf of Earning Serendipity: sharing the harvest.

It is true that the three-leaf clover is common to see. One can pass through a field and, with little observation, spot this plant. The same might be said of those who only employ the first three leaves. While such people and companies are certainly not the majority, they are not uncommon. With little observation, one can spot them amid the landscape of the marketplace. They are entrepreneurs, top executives, rising managers, and current leaders of their fields. We read of them in our magazines and newspapers. We hear them speak at events and watch them interviewed on television. We listen to their advice and seek to emulate their examples. Perhaps we are even tempted to call them the elite. Yet they are more common than one might think. They are not the elite. These who see, sow, and grow the seeds of great opportunities are the three-leaf clovers in the field. Unless they also employ the Fourth Leaf of Earning Serendipity, they will not sustain a momentum of good fortune. They are sand castles for only an hour. The tide of commerce changes, and many of their foundations are swept away.

It is only those who employ all four of the leaves of earning serendipity who are the elite, the true serendipiters. These are the ones who climb to the top of their careers or their industries and have the biggest impact in their communities, because they understand how to use innovation and initiative to sustain the momentum of good fortune in spite of unpredictable forces. Such people and companies are the four-leaf clovers in the fields before us. Like the plant that represents only one in ten thousand of the clovers in the field, they are rare. Perhaps it is appropriate, then, that Irish legend says the rare four-leaf clover is found only by those who deserve it. For the power and responsibility that comes to those who possess all Four Leaves is momentous. They are deserving of their momentum of good fortune.

Google

THE THIRD LEAF
Strategic Focus: *Growing* Seeds of Greatest Potential

It is the mark of a serendipiter to strategically focus on his sown seeds, constantly monitoring their growth and promise. To sustain any measure of good fortune, this sort of opportunity management is critical. For instance, you must always know when one opportunity must be watered less in order to give more water to another that is growing more rapidly. You must know which seeds of opportunity are not growing as you had once thought. And above all, you must know which opportunities require your greatest focus, for it is these which will ensure your greatest harvest. This is the essence of applying the Third Leaf of Earning Serendipity, and it is responsible for a brand that is so strong today it is both a noun and a verb. I am speaking of Google.

Today's leader of all search engines began in 1996 as a mere research project for Stanford PhD candidates Larry Page and Sergey Brin. While most would perhaps be singularly grateful to have just concluded their research, these two serendipiters took their findings much further. They sought to then grow this seed of great potential.

In his doctoral research, Page noted similarities between the process of "backlinking" in the World Wide Web and the process of making citations in academic publishing. He theorized that just as the credibility of an academic work is often weighted by the number and diversity of other works it cites, the importance of any given Web page could also be determined by the number of other pages to which it is linked.

Page quickly enlisted the help of math-prodigy Sergey Brin to further flesh out his theory. In this manner, he was giving greater focus to this now deep-sown seed. Together, these two serendipiters developed the system known as PageRank, named after its creator. As it so happens, their strategic focus produced a momentum of good fortune beyond their expectations. Their PageRank system began delivering far more relevant Web search results than the search engine giants of the day, Yahoo and Lycos.

Growth, from there, was rapid and before long would become more abundant then either ever considered. We might say the two had clearly seen, sown, and now grown their seed of greatest potential with great proficiency. Just one year after their first meeting, Page and Brin created the fully functional search engine named Google, a direct reference to the base number "googol," a one followed by a hundred zeros. Perhaps it too was a prophetic nod to the expansive measure of growth that would come from this once small and single seed. Their search engine soon became the standard for Stanford students and faculty and then most of Silicon Valley. From this point their story is quite familiar to many.

It was 1999, and the industrialized world was flush with investment capital—much of it attracted to the dot-coms. It was then that Page and Brin made their first attempt at monetizing Google through ad sales. While their initial efforts were marked by only fits of growth, they continued to water their deep-sown seed so it might flourish into full bloom. Perhaps they were not even sure themselves what this would look like, but of one thing we can be certain: Both were committed to strategic focus unto harvest. By 2002, sight of this harvest became clear as they introduced "relevancy" to the search ad market. We might say it was then that these wise men tangibly understood the Third Leaf of Earning Serendipity. For it was then that Google truly became the preeminent expert in the search engine model we might call "focus and discovery." One inserts a focused entry into Google in order to discover an abundance of results. It is perhaps no coincidence that this model is the very embodiment of growing seeds of greatest potential. In the same manner, the seren-dipiter *focuses* on his seed of greatest potential in order to *discover* its abundant harvest. And this is where we might say that momentum becomes all the more sustainable. Once a seed has grown large, do not additional seeds of great potential come into view? They do; and they have done so with the well-grown seed of Google.

By allowing engineers to devote 20 percent of their paid work time to the pursuit of personal projects, Google continues to germinate additional seeds that keep its harvest growing. The company's vice president of search products and user experience, Marissa

Mayer, estimates that approximately half of Google's new products are the result of this 20 percent personal time, including Gmail, Orkut, Google News, and its flagship AdSense program. By creating an environment that promotes seeing, sowing, and growing seeds of great potential, Google sustains not only its perpetual harvest but also its good fortune of being king of search engines.

Perhaps there is also a corporate lesson we might learn from this ever-growing seed of great potential. It was my father who often asserted that the most important entrepreneurial seed a company grows is the talent which represents it. Of this, Google is an excellent model worth emulating. For in the end, the seeds of greatest potential are often already within our reach: they reside, dormant, in the hearts and minds of those all around us until they are given a field in which to flourish. The leadership and the company that gives as such will find no shortage of good fortune.

References

AllBusiness.com. "What is CPM-Based Web Advertising?" www.allbusiness.com/marketing/advertising-internet-advertising/2646-1.html.

Battelle, John. "The Birth of Google." Wired Magazine, August 2005. www.wired.com/wired/archive/13.08/battelle.html.

Karp, Scott. Google AdWords: A Brief History of Online Advertising Innovation. Publishing 2.0, May 27, 2008. publishing2.com/2008/05/27/google-adwords-a-brief-history-of-online-advertising-innovation.

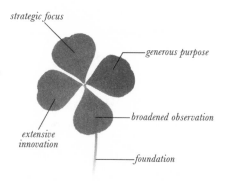

strategic focus

generous purpose

broadened observation

extensive innovation

foundation

CHAPTER 4

Generous Purpose:
Sharing the Harvest

"We should so live and labor in our time that what came to us as seed
may go to the next generation as blossom; and what came to us as
blossom may go to them as fruit. This is what we mean by progress."

—HENRY WARD BEECHER

The power of earning serendipity will enable you to see, sow, and
grow opportunities you never thought possible—opportunities in
your career or in the company that you run. But you can be certain
the best opportunities always culminate in the meeting of others'
needs. This is true whether you're a first-time sales representative or
the CEO of a Fortune 500 company.

Perhaps one might create a momentum of good fortune by regularly applying the first three leaves. She will reap success and it will afford her many things. She will climb high and be recognized by peers for her accomplishments. Yet if this person fails to continually reinvest her harvest into the success of others—if this person fails to continually share her harvest—her good fortune will be impossible to sustain. The only true momentum in today's global marketplace is the ongoing opportunity to deliver on the needs of others—to create and then sustain a harvest that improves the fortune of more than one individual or one corporate entity.

It is no coincidence that we have seen a great rise in what we've come to call corporate social responsibility, or CSR. Perhaps we are beginning to understand this fourth leaf. Has not CSR become an essential component of any company that desires to thrive? Perhaps it is so for good reason. The only way to sustain a momentum of good fortune is to continually increase the good fortune of others. This is as true for the individual as it is for the corporation.

Once you begin to reap the benefits of properly seeing, sowing, and growing seeds of opportunity, you must then be prepared to share the perpetual harvest of good fortune. The only way to accomplish this is to make generosity part of your purpose, to make generosity an integral part of the DNA of your career or company. You've heard it said that it is better to give than to receive, and I tell you nothing is more true in this world. The fortunate one works in such a way that he is always giving more than receiving. The continually fortunate company employs the same in its daily practice. This is what it means to apply a generous purpose. This is what it means to apply the Fourth Leaf of Earning Serendipity.

THE MOMENTUM OF GIVING IT AWAY

When we speak of purpose, we first think of ourselves. This is natural, and I will not tell you it is wrong. Perhaps we might say we are survivors by nature and thrivers by nurture. Yet the individual's or company's primary purpose for existence cannot begin and end with itself, for no true purpose is exclusive to self. A true purpose must include others.

Every great purpose is outside the individual. My father often asserted,

> "Show me one who works only for himself, and I'll show you short-lived success. Show me a company with self-serving practices, and I'll show you a short-lived business. In the end, *es todo acerca de personas*"—it's all about people.

I do not speak merely of the principle of reciprocity, though the fortunate one who shares his harvest with others will certainly reap the benefits of those who return his gift. I speak primarily of the principle of generosity, for the one who shares his harvest because it moves him to do so multiplies his harvest far more than he who merely makes a living by bartering.

There are many ways to explain this difference, but perhaps none is more common to our experience than the difference between the company that makes a public spectacle of a gift and the company that gives through daily practice.

One shoemaker builds a global business through quality design and craftsmanship, and in its third year of profitability formally partners with a charity in the city of its main offices. A press release is written and a grand celebration is planned, at which time a large check will be presented on a large stage to the president of the local charity. The day of the event arrives and the media are present in abundance. The event is a great success. In the following days, the big gift is written up in papers and on the Internet. The shoemaker is a generous woman, say many. She and her company have made a great impact.

Perhaps these people are right. Perhaps the company did not merely seek a large write-off in the manner that would reap them greatest publicity. Perhaps the owner did not seek only to increase favor between her company and the media, and thus secure space in which to promote a new product. Who can judge the heart of a woman and her company? Perhaps we cannot judge because publicity is part of business acumen—recognition holds inherent value in the marketplace. No, we should not judge the motives of the woman, but we can be certain about one thing: neither she nor her company embodies a generous purpose.

Giving was not a foundation of the company's design. It was carried out, not as a matter of founding practice, but rather in proportion to and in strategy with the company's increasing success. The maxim for such a person and company—and there are many like them—is this: Give when giving makes fiscal sense. Give only when it is strategic, is convenient, or requires little sacrifice. We have spoken of convenience previously. (The one who sustains a momentum of good fortune cares little for it.) Until a person sees that giving makes more fiscal sense than hoarding one's success, this person will not cultivate a perpetual harvest.

In great contrast to this woman and her company, another shoemaker launches a business with a promise to give away one pair of shoes for every pair that is purchased. He too builds a global business with quality design and craftsmanship. Yet the very fiber of his company's practice is generosity. His enterprise seeks to exist and grow in order to give shoes to those around the world who have none. Will this man and his company reap the recognition similar to that of his fellow shoemaker without public spectacle? In this age of instant information, he certainly will. Others will hear of this man's generous purpose through each purchase, and they will not only buy his shoes, they will also back his cause. All things being equal, will people not do more for this man and his company than for the first shoemaker? They will because there is a vast difference between recognition and respect.

In the world of business, we recognize those who sell well, but we respect and remember those who give well.

The one who lacks a generous purpose cares primarily for recognition.
The one with a generous purpose cares primarily for respect.

IMPACTING THE HEAD OR THE HEART

Respect reverberates and multiplies. Recognition explodes and sub-sides. I will not tell you that recognition should not be desired. For certain, one should possess it in order to advance a career, company, or cause. The worker must ensure that his boss sees his success. The company must ensure that its consumers see the effect of its product or service. The nonprofit must make its needs known. But those who sustain good fortune will not seek recognition alone. In fact, they will not seek it primarily. The fortunate understand that respect is more lasting than recognition.

A regional sales manager takes his team to the top ranks in revenue and keeps them there for three consecutive quarters. Several company executives recognize his success and wonder if he is a candidate for a higher position, perhaps the new vice president of North American sales. It is a position that will soon be vacant.

The sales manager also sees this opportunity. He has seen, sown, and grown the opportunities before him, and now it seems his seeds will reap a more-abundant harvest of opportunity. Perhaps, he tells himself, his hard work will finally pay off.

However, the question that now remains is not whether the man is deserving of recognition. The numbers speak for themselves, and for these he will be recognized as at least worthy of promotion consideration. No, the question that remains . . . the question that will determine whether this man's harvest will expand further . . . the question that will dictate whether he sustains his momentum of good fortune . . . is whether or not he has earned respect.

As the interview process begins, the wise company executives will give the man an opportunity to speak for himself, but they will then proceed to speak of those he has managed and those with whom he has done business. Do they like working with the man? Do they trust the man? Do they think he will continue to succeed? Ultimately, these questions culminate in one: Do they respect the man? Any wise executive must have reservations about the man who can get people to work for him and buy from him but cannot earn their respect.

My father once said,

> "The great difference between the recognized man and the respected man is the difference of the head and heart. The recognized man appeals to the head where things are easily forgotten. The respected man captivates the heart. *Y el corazón no se olvida*"— And the heart does not forget.

Unfortunately, the corporate world has taught us to be recognition addicts. In the corporate culture of fierce competition, we have come to believe we are our own best allies. We believe we must rely only on ourselves. We believe we can sell ourselves better than anyone else. But I tell you, these things are a great danger to one's good fortune.

The one who sustains a momentum of good fortune knows that others are far better promoters of his fortune than he is. He thus always makes certain his work includes and impacts the hearts of others. He does not work for himself alone but for all those his work touches. He is always asking, "How will my work make the biggest impact?"

It is certain that one must be aware of his past and current successes. He will be asked to give account of these on many occasions, and he must have confidence in discussing them. But this man cannot rely on his resume, for it alone will not captivate the hearts of others nor compel them to expand his harvest. Will not the sales manager fail to receive the promotion if his people reveal they do not respect him? Only the foolish executive would promote a man based solely on a paper reputation. The sales manager cannot therefore sustain his momentum of good fortune alone—no matter how much experience he brings to the table. And the same will be true of the individuals and companies who seek only recognition. One must possess respect to earn and keep earning serendipity. To do so, one must set out to perpetually share his harvest in daily practice.

THE SECURITY OF GOOD FORTUNE

A man cannot sustain a momentum of good fortune in and of himself. If he properly sees, sows, and grows the best seeds of opportunity before him, his harvest will certainly be larger than one man can consume. What the man then does with what he cannot consume—with what is more than enough—ultimately determines what sort of man he is and whether he will remain a fortunate man for long. Will he only tell others about his harvest? Will he call the media and ask them to broadcast news of it? Will he hold parties to celebrate his good fortune? If the man seeks to sustain his momentum, he will know these self-glorifying stunts will soon be forgotten, for they do not impact the hearts of others. If the man is wise, he will work harder to tangibly share his harvest with others who will enjoy its prosperity. This alone will ensure that his good fortune continues. This alone will impact the hearts of others. And those that receive of the harvest will not forget the man.

Recall the wise farmer whose land lay just off the dusty road, a mile from the small Cuban coastal town. This man exemplified that of which I speak. Through a consistent sharing of his harvest, he possessed the respect of the people of his town. This helped him protect his good fortune. Because he shared his harvest, there were always many who remained loyal to the farmer and who would not hesitate to help or support him. These townspeople protected the wise farmer's good fortune because they wanted that good fortune to remain. The farmer's good fortune was their good fortune as well. They were vested in the harvest.

What the foolish investor did not realize is that when he presented his offer to the wise farmer, he not only showed himself to be ignorant of the significance of proper sowing, he also proposed a means of business that would undermine the farmer's security of good fortune. The wise farmer understood that if he gave the investor control of the harvest, it was certain the foolish man would have forced the townspeople to purchase the crops for a greater cost than the small sum the farmer required in order to sustain his simple way of life. This would, the farmer knew, put at risk the respect the people had for him. What, then, would have happened to the farmer if he lost the respect of the townspeople and no longer had control over his harvest? In sum, he would have lost control over his good fortune. His momentum would have been halted, and he would have been helpless to regain it in the same manner in which it had existed before.

COLLABORATION IS THE KEY

It is said that you alone hold the keys to your success, but this is only true if the keys are entrusted also to others. You see, to apply the Fourth Leaf of Earning Serendipity one must be more than an initiator of momentum. One must also habitually utilize his harvest to secure his momentum and cultivate further opportunities. This is embodied in collaboration.

Many take their good fortune for granted and thus fall victim to their prosperity. With each success, they upgrade their lifestyle and consume more and more of the harvest themselves. In doing so, these people impoverish the momentum of their harvest.

There is more to consumption than meets the eye. At its core, consumption either erodes or upholds your momentum of good fortune. The wise man seeks first and foremost to use his good fortune to increase the number of those with whom he collaborates. He does not seek first to increase his own consumption.

I do not speak here of living simply, for each person must set his own standard of success and the means with which he will be satisfied to live.

I also do not speak merely of what we like to call networking. For the fortunate man is always increasing his network by the manner in which he carries himself. He does not seek relationships merely to expand a list, which he will then exploit. He seeks relationships with people who will benefit from the excess of his harvest, for he knows these people will desire his momentum to continue.

When I speak of employing collaboration in daily practice, I speak primarily of the particular purpose by which a fortunate man works. If one's primary purpose is to increase his success in order to increase his consumption, his harvest will eventually lose its security. He will make decisions for himself alone and thus keep the keys of success tightly in his own hands. Who will care that his harvest continues if none will receive ongoing benefit from it? None will care. He will have no collaboration. If he sells products, those who have purchased them will have no heartfelt reason to continue buying from him when many others offer the same. To sustain any measure of good fortune, this man will be forced to rely on his ability to constantly secure new business. If this man is merely working his way up the corporate ladder, he will be forced to continually state his case with the people for and with whom he works. He must constantly sell himself.

He will have less leverage and influence in the company than his coworker who possesses the respect of many. Yes, this coworker, who in contrast seeks primarily to include others in her harvest, will remain secure in her good fortune. Many will care that her harvest continues. Not only will she always have more opportunities budding in her field, she will also be consistently more successful if she continues to see, sow, grow, and share these opportunities. In sum, this coworker who collaborates will consistently have more good fortune than the one who seeks only the means to greater consumption.

BECOMING A SERENDIPITER

The fortunate one banks his momentum on continual impact. The fortunate company does the same. Both habitually share their harvests with others through daily practice and through success. That is why we say that a serendipiter is one who is socially conscious and inspires innovation and initiative that propels good fortune for herself and her community. While it is certain that many who receive a share of the harvest cannot return the generosity equivocally, the expanding respect of the individual or the company will ensure that two things occur:

1. People remain vested in sustaining the harvest sharer's good fortune.

2. Opportunities continue to appear before, around, beneath, and beyond the harvest sharer.

You see, the fortunate sustain their current momentum through relationship management while simultaneously creating future momentum through success management. In essence, those who sustain good fortune ensure the simultaneous growth of relationships and success. As one increases, so does the other. This is the result and strength of sharing the harvest. As relationships increase, so does success. As success increases, so do relationships. There is no way for anyone to fake the way to this momentum.

There are four principles by which the fortunate one regularly measures his proficiency of sharing the harvest in his work or organization. You must do the same if you are to sustain the momentum of good fortune you have created through the first three leaves.

THE FOUR PRINCIPLES OF WORKPLACE MOMENTUM

1. **Success that ruins relationships = false good fortune**
2. **Relationships that ruin success = forfeited good fortune**
3. **Success that builds relationships = future good fortune**
4. **Relationships that build success = frequent good fortune**

These four principles ultimately serve as authenticators of a true momentum of good fortune. The individual or company that will sustain the momentum they have created through seeing, sowing, and growing the best opportunities will also ensure that principles three and four are always occurring in greatest measure. While it is certain that ongoing illegal and immoral activity will always ensure that principles one and two are prevalent, the individual or company that continually embodies sharing the harvest will be protected in numbers. Neither will lose momentum when the majority of success builds relationships and the majority of relationships builds success.

On the other hand, the individual or company that is not embodying the Fourth Leaf of Earning Serendipity is at risk of losing the momentum from one mispurposed harvest or one mispurposed relationship. We often witness this misfortune. The employee receives a promotion to manager of his department and then forgets those who helped him produce the harvest of good fortune. In his self-consumption, he now treats these former allies as subservient. Will these people who must now answer to him work to ensure that his good fortune continues? They certainly will not. Perhaps some will even take pleasure in his misfortune.

Thus for one to employ the Fourth Leaf of Earning Serendipity—for one to ensure that he is continually sharing the harvest—he must transition from being merely an *initiator* to becoming a *collaborator*. An initiator sees, sows, and grows seeds of opportunity but cannot sustain his good fortune, for not enough people care for his harvest to continue. A collaborator sees, sows, and grows seeds of opportunity and then sustains his good fortune by ensuring that others always benefit from his success. And this is the man that I have been telling you of all along—the serendipiter.

The Initiator Versus the Serendipiter

I will now show you the three primary differences between the one who is only an initiator and the one who is both initiator and collaborator—the serendipiter—whose character you must emulate if you are to sustain good fortune.

Difference #1: *An initiator looks to increase income; a serendipiter looks to increase influence.*

It is certain the world of business is full of initiators who are wealthy people. Many have remained wealthy for years, and I tell you this is possible if one has a keen understanding of the nuances of a particular market or industry. But such people will always have their ups and downs. Such people, no matter how much money they have, will not be able to avoid great misfortunes. Some of the world's greatest moneymakers have filed for bankruptcy. Some have filed more than once. These initiators will know great misfortunes alongside their great fortunes. These people will eventually fail to sustain their momentum of good fortune because they look primarily to increase income rather than influence.

Some will say that a man with a great fortune must certainly have influence, but it is not influence that allows such a man to remain successful; it is the appeal of income. It is said that money talks, and it convinces many to help others they may or may not respect. Thus, money will also convince these same people otherwise. The wealthy man without influence will always be at risk of a mass exodus because people are only loyal to his money. The prospect of more money will often convince hangers-on to join with another or even to overtake the one with great income.

It is certain that one can increase income without influence. We see this everywhere every day. But if one is to avoid great misfor-

tunes of income, one must have an increasing measure of influence
with people.

This influence is the greatest single force in the business world
when properly obtained. I have found that what we often call influence is merely the forces of coercion, persuasion, money, or obligation. True influence is earned only through the respect of others. To
build the foundation of your momentum on any force but that of
genuine influence is to build your foundation on sand. When the
skies fall hard, only the man with much influence will remain firm.
He alone will have others willing to help uphold the walls of his
business or work. We see this every day.

The sky over the mortgage industry has fallen, and many have
faced great misfortunes. Which ones have sustained a momentum
of good fortune? The few who maintained a genuine measure of
influence among those with whom they work and serve. It is possible these few with influence will experience a slighter harvest than
in previous years. But it is also certain these maintained a harvest
when most in the industry faced only fallow ground. Are not people still buying homes? Yes, and home buyers are using the services
of those who have earned their respect and have thus maintained a
measure of influence.

It is a mistake to merely speak of success in terms of dollars and
cents. All commerce, all capital, all investment, and all advancement come through people, and therefore the one who sustains
momentum is the serendipiter who looks primarily to earn and sustain influence with the source of all income: people. With the many
who respect him, the serendipiter will have no shortage of oppor-

tunity for income in good economical times and bad. Those with whom he has influence through harvest sharing will remain loyal to his harvest. And some will share their harvest with him.

Difference #2: *An initiator leans on expanding creativity; a serendipiter leans on expanding community.*

The initiator immediately invests the abundance of his harvest into the next venture. He therefore remains in a circumstance where he must constantly differentiate himself from others. He must always find a way to create space in which he can be recognized. He is thus always in competition, and even at the top of his game he will not win every time.

The serendipiter takes a different approach and instead invests the abundance of his harvest in expanding his community. His strategy for success is to increase the body of supporters around him. In doing so, he leans on the security that comes from many people wanting him to succeed. We have touched on this subject before, but we will conclude the thought here.

What the serendipiter understands that the initiator does not is that competition (for a job, a promotion, an account, or a majority market share) can be mitigated if enough people want one competitor to succeed above all others. The fortunate one thus seeks to earn this advantage in every endeavor he pursues by continually investing his harvest in the lives of many—and he does this in a way that ensures that these people want his success and continual good fortune. This man will rarely need to ask for the support of those he's invested in, for they will take pleasure in seeing him succeed. His success will be their success.

We have already said that these people in whom the fortunate man invests will have eyes to spot great opportunities for him as well as signs of misfortune. In this way, these people will both expand his field of opportunity and shield it from harm. But there is more these people can provide for the fortunate man.

Perhaps the man is to launch a new business or expand his current one. Who will succeed against this man if he already possesses the respect of the majority of the market? None will. This man must only listen to the needs of his growing community in order to know how to sow and grow his harvest. The strongest brands in the world, such as IKEA, are expert in this skill, and it is the reason they are so difficult to supplant. Many desire their good fortune to continue, and thus the only way to topple them is to somehow take away the respect of the community. This is a difficult task steeped in failure.

Let us suppose the serendipiter is only an employee. This skill is just as effective. All things relatively equal, the employee with the greater measure of respect and support within the company will most often get the promotion, the raise, and in general, the better opportunities. Thus the employee who sustains a momentum of good fortune that propels him up the corporate ladder is most often the one who leans on a strategy of expanding his community. While he does not diminish ongoing innovation, he understands that his greatest security is found in a growing foundation of advocates.

Difference #3: *An initiator desires to make a mark;*
a serendipiter desires to leave a legacy.

The final measure of the purpose of an individual or a company is the culmination of its actions. The initiator's work makes only a temporary mark that will eventually wear off. The ultimate effect of his harvest is not unlike that of a greatly anticipated party. Many will speak of it in the days leading up to it. Many will arrange their schedules and leverage their resources to be participants in it. Yet in the weeks and months after the great party, the effect begins to wear off. Before long, it is forgotten. It is the same for the initiator. Once he is no longer working, no longer initiating, the mention of him or his company brings memories of good fortune but not continued, tangible good fortune. He has thus left only a mark on the mind—a memory—that fades in ever-increasing measure as time passes. Perhaps it is simplest to say that the initiator has an impact only on a company or an industry. He does not have an impact on humanity.

The serendipiter takes a different approach and thus has a much different effect. He seeks, ultimately, to leave a legacy that will bring continued good fortune to many lives after he or his company is gone. He thus employs a strategy to collaborate in greatest fashion with a select few who will not only benefit from his good fortune but also be prepared to continue cultivating a perpetual harvest in the months and years after he has gone. This extra measure is not a complicated one, as the serendipiter is already using a generous purpose to expand his foundation of supporters. This extra step to secure a legacy of good fortune is merely a matter of investing

a deeper measure into a select few with whom he already collaborates. Thus his legacy of good fortune—and the means by which he
earns it—is first passed to a smaller number of supporters in order
that they themselves will begin producing a similar harvest of good
fortune. The serendipiter understands that it is not his name that
must reverberate after he is gone but rather the good fortune his
name has earned. This is an effect many experience, but they do
not know it is so. I tell you there are many people we are not aware
of who set in motion a legacy of good fortune that many still enjoy
today.

This is the ultimate effect of the one who applies the Four
Leaves of Earning Serendipity: a transcendent harvest for future
generations to enjoy. My father always said,

> "In the end, there is only individual
> effort, *pero propósito no individual*"—
> but no individual purpose.

If anyone will create and sustain a legacy of good fortune, he
must ultimately join other fortunate ones in the business of better-
ing the world. This is the mark of a serendipiter.

IKEA

THE FOURTH LEAF
Generous Purpose: *Sharing* the Harvest

It is perhaps appropriate that the company that exemplifies the Fourth Leaf of Earning Serendipity was itself born of a gift. In 1943, at the age of seventeen, founder Ingvar Kamprad received a small monetary reward from his father for excelling in his studies. With this gift, Kamprad formally established IKEA, taking the name from his own initials and the first letters of the farm, Elmtaryd, and the village, Agunnaryd, where he grew up. In the same generous spirit that allowed him to first launch his company, Kamprad continues to Share the Harvest.

There is much that might be said of the lengths to which IKEA has gone to share its harvest, but nothing is perhaps more compelling than the company's reaction to a horrific occurrence that took place in the mid-nineties.

It was in 1995 when the world first heard of the murder of twelve-year-old child labor activist Iqbal Masih. The tale that was then revealed of his bonded indenture horrified the world.

At the age of four, Iqbal had been sold into bonded labor to a local carpet weaver for the sum of six hundred rupees, or about twelve dollars, which his family had borrowed to pay for his older brother's wedding. He was tied to a loom and forced to work fourteen-hour days in order to repay that original debt, which due to the addition of interest and charges for the boy's food and board, grew to about $260 by the time Iqbal, at age ten, was freed by the Bonded Labor Liberation Front of Pakistan.

The boy then became a poster child for the hideous labor conditions and practices in the factories of his region and beyond. Iqbal lectured on the subject all around the world, and he was personally responsible for freeing hundreds of children from forced labor before being shot and killed while riding his bicycle in his village in Pakistan. Though his murder remains officially unsolved, he was thought by many to have been killed by the "Carpet Mafia" for his work as an activist against it. Here is where IKEA entered the story.

It was discovered that the factory at which Iqbal was once enslaved sold rugs to IKEA, as well as many other companies. Upon hearing this, Ingvar Kamprad and his IKEA executives immediately took action that would bring to light its foundational commitment to sharing the harvest.

First, IKEA did the obvious. It looked internally at its own supply chain and began addressing the problem from within, taking all steps necessary to ensure that an IKEA product never again would be created by manufacturers that exploited children.

IKEA then solidified a commitment to eradicate the problem at its root. The company partnered with UNICEF to create a program to help prevent child labor by changing the conditions that led to child labor in the first place: namely, poverty, hunger, and illiteracy.

Today, this same program serves more than five hundred villages in India's Carpet Belt, an area with a population in excess of 1.3 million. IKEA has further helped to establish self-help groups for women, which aid them in creating savings of their own and provide them access to micro-loans so tragedies like Iqbal's never happen again.

Acknowledging that poverty was often the result of the onset of illness, IKEA and UNICEF also worked with the World Health Organization to establish a five-year vaccination program in the region, vaccinating almost three hundred thousand women and children from three thousand villages in the period from 2002 to 2007.

Perhaps you are tempted to consider IKEA's actions somewhat common among the socially responsible Western companies of today. I will tell you that its dedication to sharing the harvest is no common commitment. IKEA has consistently been a leader in taking steps to be a company that makes the world a better place. It does so by keeping a commitment to regularly seeking the advice and assistance of experts in many arenas like the environment, wise energy use, fair trade, and ethical workplace standards. We might say that long before social responsibility became the buzzword it is today, IKEA was already holding to the standard. It now sets the standard in many ways, and I must remind you that this is by no means a cheap investment. In doing so IKEA has become a model of proficiency in sharing the harvest. It is thus clear why its harvest is both perpetual and well earned.

It is quite appropriate that the small monetary reward that the boy Kamprad received and then shared through IKEA has returned a momentum of good fortune a millionfold. IKEA is repeatedly named to *Forbes* magazine's "Top 100 Companies to Work For" and was recently named to *Ethisphere*'s "World's Most Ethical Companies" list. And perhaps most appropriate of all is that Ingvar Kamprad, a boy who began by selling matchsticks from his bicycle, is today the richest man in the world.

References

IKEA Group. "IKEA Full History." www.ikea.com/ms/en_GB /about_ikea_new/about/history/fullhistory.html.

IKEA Group. "IKEA History—How it all Began." www.ikea.com /ms/en_GB/about_ikea_new/about/history/index.html.

Komal, Chary. "IKEA, Social and Environmental Responsibility Initiatives." ICFAI Center for Management Research, 2006. Case Code BECG058.

Liss, Mona. "IKEA Named to 'World's Most Ethical Companies' List by Ethisphere Magazine." CSRwire, May 11, 2007. www.csrwire.com/ News/8491.html.

Liss, Mona. "IKEA Named to Fortune's 2007 '100 Best Companies To Work For' List for Third Consecutive Year." CSRwire, January 9, 2007. www.csrwire.com/News/7212.html.

Thomas Edison and the Four Leaves

I will now tell you of a man who employed the Four Leaves throughout his life. The harvest of his work is still enjoyed by millions of people today, even though he died more than seventy-five years ago. I have no doubt you are already somewhat familiar with his biography. But if perhaps you are not, then you have certainly been illuminated by the many shared harvests of this great inventor, entrepreneur, and serendipiter.

SEEING WITH CIRCULAR VISION

When we think of Thomas Alva Edison, perhaps most think of the lightbulb or the phonograph or the X-ray. And while these inventions certainly placed Mr. Edison's name into the public consciousness, it was his work on the telegraph that initiated his momentum of good fortune. For it was his ability to see a small seed of opportunity that put into motion the many great harvests that were to come.

Edison was only a teenager when he worked as a telegraph operator on the night shift. He accepted the night-shift position because the slower evenings offered him time to study and perform what he called "midnight experiments." He would bring his experiments into the telegraph station and work on them during the downtimes. It was there his circular vision was put to use. The combination of his amazing mind and his proximity to the equipment focused his attention on how the telegraph worked, and there in that station, Edison saw an opportunity to make it work better. Most would not question something that was already working well, but a serendipiter like Edison would—and did.

At the age of sixteen, he unveiled his first authentic invention: the automatic repeater, which transmitted telegraph signals between unmanned stations, allowing the recipient to translate the messages at his own speed and convenience. No longer did the operator have to jump at the first clicks of Morse code and hope he heard correctly. An operator—one very much like Edison, who liked experimenting rather than manning his post—could make use of the repeater to ensure that the entire message was accurate.

Through circular vision, Edison observed inefficiencies in the system and then saw an opportunity to improve upon them. But as it so happened, his circular vision was so astute that he saw more than one way. Over the course of his life, Edison would be granted 186 patents for the telegraph and telephony.

The automatic repeater revolutionized the telegraph industry. But it was more than mere invention—it was innovation. There is a difference, which the serendipiter understands: an invention is the creation of something new; an innovation is the creation or renewal of something that revolutionizes a community, a city, a world.

There is power in innovation, and it is the skill of seeing with circular vision that allows one to move beyond mere invention and tap into it. Edison was gifted in this skill.

SOWING ENTREPRENEURIAL SEEDS

Edison expanded his good fortune through extensive innovation. As we have said, he introduced to the world the lightbulb, the phonograph, and the X-ray. But Edison's most important invention was one that you perhaps have never heard of.

In 1874, Edison invented the quadruplex telegraph, which allowed the transmission of two signals in each direction down one wire. As a mere invention, this certainly wasn't more important than other inventions that preceded and succeeded it. In fact, multichannel lines were already in use at that time, and one might argue that this invention was inevitable. No, what sets the quadruplex telegraph apart is not the invention itself but how Edison put to use the harvest that he reaped from its sale. We might say that this particular seed he sowed was purely an entrepreneurial seed—one that would grow to harvest in order to reap and share a greater harvest.

Edison sold the quadruplex telegraph to Western Union for the sum of $10,000—a large sum at that time. He then used the proceeds to establish an entirely new way of doing business. The $10,000 went to establish the very first industrial research laboratory in history, the famous facilities in Menlo Park, New Jersey. Flowing from this facility was the technological lifeblood of the twentieth century—the first practical lightbulb, the microphone, the phonograph, the subway, and much more. Some four hundred patents came out of the Menlo Park Laboratory between 1876 and 1884 alone. But equally important to the future of American industry was the new business and innovation model that Edison presented to the world.

To Menlo Park he brought the best and brightest thinkers in each relevant field together under one roof in order to work in concert toward creating a bigger and brighter future. Together, a Swiss clock maker, a German glassblower, a mathematician, machinists, carpenters, and a host of lab assistants created the future through seeing, sowing, and growing entrepreneurial seeds. They then shared the harvest of those seeds with the world.

By 1884, following the death of his wife and increased periods of absence, Edison finally closed the lab at Menlo Park and moved to New York. Yet he would continue to apply the model he developed at Menlo Park, as would countless others. Edison would go on to found, cofound, or acquire more than 150 companies in more than a dozen industries, including at least one you have heard of, perhaps: General Electric. It is clear that this man possessed in abundance the skill of sowing entrepreneurial seeds, seeds that changed the world.

GROWING SEEDS THROUGH FOCUS

The mere ability to sow entrepreneurial seeds was not the whole of the secret to Mr. Edison's momentum of good fortune. Perhaps his greatest talent lay in growing the seeds of greatest potential through focus. Without this skill, his good fortune and the perpetual harvests would have been short-lived.

Biographers of Edison often refer to the Edisonian Method as that of "trial and error." Edison defined a problem, such as creating a durable filament for the incandescent lightbulb, and then worked toward a solution to the problem through the scientific method: observation, hypothesis, experiment, and analysis. When something wasn't working, he would leave that seed to die in order to give greater focus to those seeds that showed greater promise. He would, in essence, water selectively and through careful deliberation.

Still, it's on the level of enterprise that Edison's skill of strategic focus truly shone. He would not stop with the mere seeing and sowing of a seed; he continued by ensuring the seed's maximum growth. He created the first practical lightbulb, and then an entire power-delivery system to make it practical. It is certain the bulb was a vision (seeing) and application (sowing) of a genius seed. Yet without the strategic focus (growing) to see it transition into a commercial enterprise, how many people would have ever benefited from it? Without the power to make it glow, the lightbulb would have simply been an expensive piece of glass.

It is so that without his proficiency for growing seeds through strategic focus, Edison would have reaped only a small fraction of his harvest. It is good fortune for us that even today, he still possesses the record for the most American patents awarded to one serendipitous individual—1,093—with hundreds more international patents to his credit.

SHARING THE HARVEST

We've now seen how the first three leaves of earning serendipity were at the foundation of Edison's momentous work. Yet without his ability to apply the principle of generous purpose—the fourth leaf—I daresay the world would not know the good fortune of his harvest.

I do not speak merely of the GE Foundation and the tens of millions of dollars it has donated toward scholarships and grants. It is certain this speaks of the legacy of Edison's generous purpose, but I tell you there is an earlier and perhaps more-lucid example of how this man's application of the Fourth Leaf of Earning Serendipity greatly expanded his momentum of good fortune.

I have told you how Thomas Edison was working as a telegraph operator in his teen years, and how this experience created an initial momentum for the work he did throughout his life. Yet I did not tell you how the young Edison happened to find himself in that place at that time.

It is said the young Edison used to frequent the Mount Clemens Train Depot, a tiny station between Port Huron and Detroit. While there one day, he spotted a three-year-old boy by the name of Jimmie Mackenzie wandering onto the train tracks. Certain lore would have us believe Edison rushed out onto the tracks and pulled little Jimmie to safety as a train barreled toward them. While no one living is quite sure whether this is true, it is certain the young Edison did fetch the small boy off the tracks and move him to a safe place.

The boy, it turns out, was the son of J. U. Mackenzie, who happened to be the depot stationmaster. Mr. Mackenzie was so grateful for Edison's intervention, he offered to teach him to use the telegraph.

Is it mere coincidence that Edison's random act of kindness, his generous purpose, was rewarded in such a serendipitous manner? This was no happenstance. Edison's proficiency with the fourth leaf—even at a young age—changed not only the course of his life but also the course of the world.

I tell you once again that all around you are seeds of opportunity to be seen, sown, grown, and shared. Are you skilled enough to spot them and willing enough to share them? The world is more fortunate when serendipiters like Edison come along.

The great Thomas Edison died with 12 million dollars in his estate, most of that in property. For certain, he made and lost millions of dollars in his lifetime, constantly putting his resources into seeing, sowing, growing, and sharing the opportunities before him. And to the end, good fortune was on his side. Now his good fortune is ours to enjoy and share. Who will be like him?

Perhaps one of Edison's dearest friends, Henry Ford, summed up this serendipiter best when he said the following:

Mr. Edison was comfortably well off. He always had what he needed. But he was not a moneymaker . . . his own portion was a mere nothing compared with the wealth he created for the world.

It is clear that this man was one who knew the good fortune available to those who see, sow, grow, and share the opportunities available to us all. A world with more Edisons is without question a better world.

References

Beals, Gerald. "The Biography of Thomas Edison." Thomas Edison.com, 1999. www.thomasedison.com/biography.html.

Bellis, Mary. "Biography of Thomas Edison." About.com. inventors.about.com/od/estartinventors/a/Edison_Bio.htm.

Bellis, Mary. "Thomas Edison Patent List." About.com. inventors.about.com/library/inventors/bledisonpatents.htm.

National Park Service. "Don't Believe Everything You Read in a Textbook!" November 5, 2004. www.nps.gov/archive/edis/edifun/edifun_4andup/faqs_fables.htm#money.

SECTION THREE

THE HARVEST

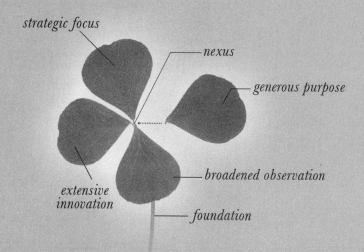

strategic focus

nexus

generous purpose

extensive innovation

broadened observation

foundation

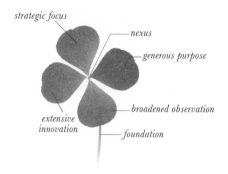

strategic focus
nexus
generous purpose
broadened observation
extensive innovation
foundation

CHAPTER 7

Leaping Ahead

"The invariable mark of wisdom is to see
the miraculous in the common."

—RALPH WALDO EMERSON

You have no doubt noticed that we have skipped two chapters. It is for good reason, for the one who learns to create and sustain a momentum of good fortune possesses the power to leap ahead.

Serendipity does not follow the rules of typical progress, which says we must climb one rung or take one step at a time as we move toward a better fortune. No, serendipity contains the power to take one step and leap three, four, even ten steps ahead—to see, sow, grow, and share one opportunity and dramatically change your fortune. Within serendipity is the power to catapult a life in an instant. Earning serendipity is about tapping into that power.

I do not speak of the lottery winners who squander their winnings as quickly as they win them. I speak here of the one who does not merely take a job but of the one who makes a job. I speak of the one who does not give to benefit herself but rather gives to benefit another. I speak of the one who does not wait for opportunity but rather seeks it out, knowing full well that one opportunity seized rightly can change a life forever. This wise one will multiply his good fortune with each step he takes. This is the power of serendipity, which he has earned. Once on his side, it is then his to squander or sustain. If he remains wise, he will do all that is necessary to keep serendipity on his side for all of his life and will not sell, forfeit, or trade this leverage for anything. He is like the immigrant of whom we have already spoken who knows that no earthly treasure contains the power of one great opportunity.

It is true, we have said, that the immigrant trusts that great opportunities are all around him, in both obvious and obscure measure. Through keen observation he is always searching for these valuable treasures. It is he who then discovers

- Opportunities in common, menial tasks
- Opportunities in requests for help
- Opportunities in small acts of kindness or sacrifice
- Opportunities in new relationships
- Opportunities in everyday conversations
- Opportunities in simple transactions
- Opportunities where no one else sees opportunities

It is in this way—through keen awareness and constant searching—that the best seeds continually come into view and offer the immigrant the power to change his fortune quickly and in exponential measure.

However, it is not merely observation or even his primal motivation to survive that sets the wise immigrant apart from the average man. In the end, it is his boundless field of opportunity that gives him the greatest advantage in grasping the good fortune that reaches out to him.

This wise man does not specify those whom he will serve—he serves all that come into his days. He does not specify the jobs he will give himself to—he allows his days to illuminate the work before him that must be done. He does not specify the field from which his opportunities will spring—the world is his field and opportunities can thus come from anywhere at any time. Unfortunately, many of the immigrant's neighbors neither believe nor behave in the same manner.

TO BE BOUNDLESS

Those raised in the United States are prone to miss sight of many opportunities simply because there are so many before us. We are also prone to drop many opportunities through apathy, laziness, or busyness. It is certain we alone are responsible for these lost opportunities, but perhaps the manner by which we are trained to see has been an ignorant accomplice.

In many ways we are taught to narrow our sight at a young age. If not by high school, certainly by college, the vast majority of us are asked to choose the field in which all our opportunities will appear. We study this field, write essays about this field, and practice working in this field where we are further educated about the opportunities within the narrow line of sight that we have chosen. We become myopic in this process. We limit our line of sight, limit the opportunities that we might discover. I have found it to be more true than not.

Perhaps most do not mean it to be so, but in a place of unlimited opportunity, we are typically trained to see, sow, and grow opportunities in one small field—and then only rarely to share the harvest those opportunities might create. Thus, most enter the workforce as twentysomethings with only a small landscape into which they might apply the Four Leaves of Earning Serendipity. These individuals might still learn to hone the tools necessary to reap an abundant harvest, but their harvest will never be as abundant as it could be because it will be contained in a small space. Unless they expand the boundaries of their fields, they will not see enough opportunity to maximize their harvests. Perhaps such people would do best to learn from the immigrant and his cousin, the entrepreneur.

THE IMMIGRANT AND THE ENTREPRENEUR

This immigrant man of whom we have spoken is perhaps most like the one we call an entrepreneur—I do not speak of the one who aspires to be an entrepreneur but rather the one who has proven through many diverse endeavors to be so. It is this wise entrepreneur who is skilled in creating something from nothing. He does not find opportunity in that which none saw opportunity before. This one operates much like the immigrant, without boundaries on the field of opportunities before him. His endeavors are not industry specific, economically specific, or socially specific; they are only opportunity specific. The best opportunities win over his eyes and then his energies, no matter where they originate.

Unlike the masses, the immigrant and the entrepreneur are not motivated to discover the perfect job, the perfect salary, or the perfect industry. Both are singularly motivated to discover great opportunity. The field before them is nothing less than the whole of the universe, without boundaries, expectations, or rules of engagement. Through different but equally effective means, these wise ones continually prove three things to be true.

Maxim #1: *Great opportunities are rare only to those who cannot see them.*

The immigrant proves that great opportunities are abundant time and again through his ability to see past the social, political, or economical labels placed on the opportunities all around him.

The secret of the immigrant is that he does not idealize his work. Instead of wading in the waters of half commitment until something finally moves him, he dives headlong into every opportunity he accepts, knowing that many opportunities are hidden behind the labels a culture or society gives to them. Furthermore, he does not see opportunity and then seek out another to sow its seed. He immediately goes about sowing the opportunity with his own hands dirtied in the soil before him, then growing it, for he knows that it is only in this way that he can maintain control of his fortune.

It has been said by some that immigrants are adverse to the economy, but the opposite is true. Immigrants are creating companies and jobs at a rate that outpaces the native population. They are seizing more opportunities and in doing so, creating more for themselves and others.

A now classic article by Bronwyn Lance of the Alexis de Tocqueville Institution provided surprising research that supports this immigrant wisdom.

> In an attempt to quantify the contributions of immigrants to America's industrial cutting edge, the Alexis de Tocqueville Institution (AdTI) completed a 1996 study that used a well-known indicator of technological innovation—issuance of new patents—to measure immigrants' inventiveness and spirit of enterprise. Examining 250 recently issued U.S. patents chosen at random, AdTI found that over 19 percent of the patents in a random sample of 48 were issued to immigrants alone or to immigrants collaborating with U.S.-born coinventors. This is over twice immigrants' proportion of the U.S. population. The immigrant inventors identified in the study included researchers, executives, entrepreneurs, and an MIT professor. Four started their own businesses, generating over 1,600 jobs.[4]

You have heard it said that great opportunities are rare, but this is true only to those who do not have eyes to see or tools to sow, grow, and share them. This the wise immigrant knows: Great opportunities are always reaching for you. The one who sustains good fortune will learn to reach back.

Maxim #2: *The field of opportunities is bound by time but not by space.*

It is said that fences are freeing, but I tell you this adage does not apply to opportunity. Once a man says to himself, "Opportunities cannot come from here or there," he has forfeited a portion of his power to affect his good fortune. The secret of the entrepreneur is that he does not place expectations on the sources of opportunity. His good fortune can thus be increased from a vast number of means. Great opportunity can come from anywhere. I will now tell you another story, which was told to me, that demonstrates the abundance of opportunities.

The wise entrepreneur stood in line at the market, and while he was thinking of the dinner he would prepare that night for his bride, he was keenly aware that perhaps good fortune reached for him from that very place where he stood. Just then the time came for the elderly man in front of him to pay, and this old man realized he could not find his money. "I had it right here," he said, pointing to his cardigan pocket.

"Perhaps it fell out while you shopped," the wise man replied. "We will go look for it together, but in the meantime, please let me pay for your groceries so these good people behind us can also buy theirs."

The elderly man was reluctant but accepted the wise man's generous offer. Together the two then retraced the elderly man's steps and discovered his wallet at the foot of the vegetable stand.

"I cannot thank you enough for your kindness," the elderly man said. "You do not know me, and yet you helped me twice in less than five minutes."

"It was no problem at all, my friend," the wise man replied. "I can only trust that in the day my wallet goes missing, someone will do the same for me."

The elderly man paused a moment, grinned, and then replied, "Well, young man, perhaps this day has come."

"I am not sure what you mean, sir. My wallet is right here."

"Well, I do not mean it in that way . . . but there is certainly a way I can repay you this day."

"You do not need to repay me, sir," replied the wise man.

"Still, I'd like to if you don't mind so much. You see, I do not mean to meddle in your business, but I overheard you earlier talking on your phone. You were speaking, I believe, to the owner of the painted brick building on Oakmont Avenue about a purchase price that you cannot agree on."

"Yes, you are right," replied the wise man. "He is a kind man, but I cannot convince him to see that what I offer him is fair—even more than what the market dictates. Still, I would love to purchase the property. It is the perfect spot for a business I have already started."

"Well," began the old man, "this man to whom you were speaking happens to be my closest friend. He and I have known one another for more than sixty years, from way back to our days in the army together. He is a good man and will sell you this property for the price you offer if he knows what sort of man you are. I will tell him tonight of your kindness to me, and he will call you tomorrow morning. I can be so sure of what I say because I originally loaned him the money to purchase the property many years ago. While he returned the money to me a few years later, he has always felt the building was as much mine as his."

"I do not know what to say," said the wise man. "Your offer is worth far more than the few dollars I have given to you. I do not deserve it."

"Young man," the older one began, "I have always said that no kindness goes unreturned. Most would have overlooked the opportunity to help me and they would have done so because they saw no value in helping an old, forgetful man find his wallet. Such people act only out of their desire to help themselves. You helped me out of no such desire and your kindness was returned tenfold. This is the way of a world most never see."

Maxim #3: You are your most immediate and ongoing opportunity.

My father used to tell me,

"The wise man forfeits his fortune when he does not trust himself."

When I was younger, I believed this to mean I must merely develop confidence in my skills. Now that I am older and have watched wise men forfeit their good fortune unnecessarily, I have come to see that I was only touching the surface of the wisdom my father shared with me. This wisdom has more to do with one's willingness and skill to see, sow, grow, and share opportunities from a three-pillared foundation of individual purpose rather than practicality or profit. To do this, one must know and trust one's self. Perhaps we might say in today's terminology that one must know and trust his brand.

We speak often of branding and brand management, and these are far too often caught up in the activity of creating and sustaining a marketplace veneer that a company believes will be most acceptable to the world and will be most profitable in the world. This is a sandy foundation that will prohibit a company from sustaining a momentum of good fortune. From this foundation, a company will pursue opportunities from the wrong vantage point, for reasons that do not align with reality. The larger the company grows, the more difficult it will become to manage the facade. The same is true for the individual.

It is tempting in our digital world to trust in someone you have only created yourself to be. The prevalence of blogging, Twittering, and Web-based social networking sites readily supports the creation and sustenance of a personal brand that cannot be maintained without losing sight of the opportunities before you that are most fitting and momentous. To go this way for long is to undermine your ability to sustain good fortune, for what man truly desires a fortune that does not fulfill him?

The point here is simple but profound: There must be alignment between who you are (your true personal brand) and the opportunities you pursue. If there is not, you will overlook those opportunities you must not miss, and instead see, sow, and grow less-significant opportunities that support your veneer brand. In the end, the good fortune you might receive is not befitting of you and therefore disenchanting. It is not meant for you but rather for the veneer of you that you created. To avoid this common fate, the one who creates and sustains good fortune ensures that there is alignment between who he is and what he pursues. This alignment is something both the wise immigrant and wise entrepreneur know well.

Perhaps surprising is that neither the immigrant nor the entrepreneur considers establishing their personal brands to be of primary importance. Instead, they understand that the opportunities they have seen, sown, grown, and shared will establish a personal brand for them. In this way, who they are (their personal brands) is embodied in the seeds they have given themselves to. The opportunities they pursue define them. This, after all we have said thus far, must not be missed.

YOU ARE OPPORTUNITY

I tell you that in the end, your life's work is nothing more than the accumulation of opportunities you have pursued. Many will say, "I am this or that; it is who I am," but by their actions we know them differently. We ask, "Do their opportunities support this claim they make? Can this personal brand be verified?" Unfortunately, often the brand cannot. In this way, we are often a people who want for things—for an identity and a life's work—which we are unwilling or unable to see, sow, grow, and share. Does not even this book cater to this quality?

Perhaps you purchased this book hoping you'd discover the secret to good fortune in a business that is not as you desire it to be, or a secret to becoming the successful person you currently are not. It is for good reason you invested your money. It is for these reasons I wrote the book. But I must warn you now, as we near the end of our time together and the beginning of yours, that the effect of applying the Four Leaves of Earning Serendipity will be momentous.

While no one can say whether you will improve your fortune today or tomorrow, it is certain that your fortune will improve, and in exponential measure. You see, the only true way to change a career or company is through new opportunities seen and seized. When you set out, as the immigrant and the entrepreneur, to primarily seek and seize the best opportunities around you—giving no thought to what brand you might create—you will add to your good fortune with each opportunity rightly pursued. When this activity—this earning serendipity—is repeated day upon day, week upon week, you will find yourself surrounded by a field of good fortune growing unto harvest. This field will be a field uniquely yours. Share it and it will remain yours. I have told you before that this field has always been there—it has been reaching for you since the day you first opened your eyes. Perhaps you have not yet seen it until now. Still, the past is no matter. In seeing today, you now possess a power to change your fortune forever. Use this power for good, and it will not lose its momentum. It is as my father has always said:

"Good fortune stays with the good.
Para ello no puede traicionarse"—
For it cannot betray itself.

The Workplace Serendipity Quiz

....

The key to the first steps of every climb is an understanding of one's current standing. I am certain that having now completed the book, you must wonder where you stand with serendipity. Are you earning it? Are you a serendipiter or are you missing the magic all around you? Perhaps you have a sense you're already doing well. Perhaps your sense is quite the opposite. From my experience of the many who've already taken the quiz, you are probably somewhat right about your standing, and somewhat wrong. We will settle the matter here.

What you will learn from your results will guide you in your efforts to master the Four Leaves of Earning Serendipity. It will reveal the extent of your entrepreneurial mind-set. It will highlight your personal combination of entrepreneurial skills that will enable you to build a momentum of good fortune and contribute to a progressive workplace brimming with innovation and a new tradition of success.

I make only one request of you as you complete the Workplace Serendipity Quiz. It is this: take it as truly as you can. One's tendency—everyone's tendency—is to take the test in the manner in which he thinks he ought to take it. That is to say, he answers the questions with his potential in mind instead of his reality. This sort of action will only ensure that the quiz is of no value to you. I thus strongly encourage you to avoid this path.

Instead, answer the questions as you would if a polygraph were attached to you. When the question pertains to something you have not yet experienced, do your best to put yourself in those shoes. What would you do—in your current skin and standing—in that situation?

If you find it difficult to take this quiz truly, I offer another suggestion. Take the quiz yourself and then allow one close to you—one who knows you and is not known to pull punches when addressing you—to take it for you. Then compare the answers and scores. Perhaps the one close to you knows you more truly than you know yourself. I would not rule this out. It is often the case—perhaps more often than we'd like to admit.

There is one more detail I must share with you now. These questions and their subsequent answers are written in such a way that makes it difficult to cheat on the quiz. In some cases the answers that seem most appropriate are actually the lowest-scoring answers. I do not tell you this to challenge your insight. I tell you this to discourage you from cheating. What good will it do you to answer according to hope or fantasy? Will you embody these same qualities and skills in the real world of business? You will not. You will work and do business just as you do now. Thus, I ask you to take the quiz in real time. You will be all the more fortunate for it, for with an honest assessment, one can know where creating and sustaining a momentum of good fortune begins.

To help you further in this direction, the quiz concludes with scoring summaries that offer you further insight into your current standing. They will help you ascertain what is helping and hindering your ability to earn serendipity. Your particular summary will also give you tips for taking the first steps toward sustaining a momentum of good fortune in your career.

I will make one final suggestion. It is said that the man who walks with the wise, grows wise, and the friend of fools becomes a fool himself.[5] Do not our experiences prove this to be true? In light of this, here then is my suggestion: Encourage those with whom you associate on a regular basis to also take this quiz and then compare your scores. If it suits you better to do this online, complete the quiz at www.earningserendipity.com or by using the Facebook Earning Serendipity application at http://apps.facebook.com/earningserendipity/. The question you are seeking to answer is this: Are your friends and associates helping or hindering your ability to earn serendipity? It has been my experience over and over again that those who associate themselves with people of equal or greater Serendipity Quotients (SQs) will find it much easier to sustain or increase their momentum of good fortune. And those who associate themselves only with people whose SQs are lower will consistently find it difficult to create or sustain a momentum of good fortune.

Where and with whom do you stand? Let us now discover—and then let us take the first steps to a more abundant, perpetual harvest.

Answer all questions honestly, based on your current standing and not where you'd like to be. Once you are finished, tally your total score based on the legend at the end of the quiz. With your score, or SQ, locate the appropriate summary to learn what it indicates about you and your ability to earn serendipity.

1. **You take a new job and are ready to quit within three months. You conclude . . .**

        A—Bad break
        B—Bad decision
        C—Good lesson
        D—I'll do better next time

2. **You're pushing a critical deadline at a job you love, and your boss delegates a menial but time-consuming task to you. You . . .**

> A—Pile the task on with the rest and hope for the best
> B—Try to reason your boss out of giving the task to you
> C—Accept the task and then delegate it to someone else
> D—Take a stand and refuse the task

3. **You've just landed a long-sought promotion after five years with a company when an industry competitor offers you a higher position with a significantly higher salary. You . . .**

> A—Take the money and run
> B—Use the offer to build your case for more money with your current company
> C—Turn the offer down on the principle of loyalty
> D—Entertain the offer and see what unfolds

4. **To everyone's surprise, at a year-end party you receive a large monetary award over a more-deserving, highly respected coworker. You . . .**

> A—Publicly refuse the bonus and ask that it be given to your coworker
> B—Take the bonus and privately split it with your coworker
> C—Take the bonus and publicly acknowledge your coworker's hard work
> D—Do nothing because "you win some, you lose some"

5. **You've invested ten years in a company you believe in when it becomes obvious that executives are fast-tracking the VP's dull nephew for a position you've earned. You . . .**

> A—Quietly but quickly look for another job
> B—Verify your observation with coworkers before doing anything
> C—Strap on your gloves and take the matter to the top
> D—Continue doing excellent work in hopes the executives rethink their plan

6. **You're working long hours but earning well into six figures when an old friend asks you to help with the launch of a brilliant new company. Your help will require at least twenty hours a week and produce no immediate income. You . . .**

> A—Keep your income-generating work the top priority and graciously turn down the offer
> B—Offer to help "as you have time"
> C—Say yes and find a way to help
> D—Explain your situation and find someone else to help in your place

7. **You've invested fifteen years in a solid career, but you have a brilliant, highly marketable idea for a new business that is time sensitive. You . . .**

> A—Invest a month giving due diligence to the business idea
> B—Quit your job and jump after the opportunity before the window closes
> C—Stay on the path you've spent fifteen years forging
> D—Try to launch the new business while initially sustaining your current career

8. **Your employer is cutting back, and you're given the option to stay on part-time or cut your losses and move on. You love your company and your job. You . . .**

> A—Cut your losses and start calling your company's competitors
>
> B—Stay on part-time and start planning your next endeavor
>
> C—Build a compelling case for the company keeping you full-time
>
> D—Stay on part-time and look for a good full-time position

9. **A wealthy relative dies and leaves you $50K. You . . .**

> A—Throw a close-knit dinner party and ask for suggestions on how to use the money
>
> B—Buy something you'd never buy with your own money and save/invest the rest
>
> C—Buy something nice and give the rest to your favorite charity
>
> D—Pay off debt and disperse the rest among your closest supporters

10. **A great opportunity comes your way, but the timing is bad and the cost is far more than you can afford. You . . .**

> A—Curse the circumstances that make the opportunity impossible to pursue
>
> B—Throw caution to the wind, borrow the money, and go for it
>
> C—Weigh the backlash and pursue the opportunity if the sacrifice is not too great
>
> D—Wait to see whether fate gives you another nudge in that direction

Workplace Serendipity Quiz

Point system for your Serendipity Quotient (SQ):

1A = 1 point	6A = 1 point
1B = 3 points	6B = 3 points
1C = 4 points	6C = 4 points
1D = 2 points	6D = 2 points
2A = 1 point	7A = 2 points
2B = 3 points	7B = 3 points
2C = 4 points	7C = 1 point
2D = 2 points	7D = 4 points
3A = 1 point	8A = 3 points
3B = 3 points	8B = 2 points
3C = 2 points	8C = 4 points
3D = 4 points	8D = 1 point
4A = 1 point	9A = 4 points
4B = 4 points	9B = 2 points
4C = 2 points	9C = 1 point
4D = 3 points	9D = 3 points
5A = 3 points	10A = 1 point
5B = 1 point	10B = 3 points
5C = 4 points	10C = 4 points
5D = 2 points	10D = 2 points

Workplace Serendipity Quiz

....

If your SQ is 36–40 . . .

You possess proficiency with at least two of the Four Leaves of good fortune in your career. You are a serendipiter in at least some respect, if not in full force. You have, therefore, certainly experienced a streak of good luck before today. Now, the only thing potentially standing between you and a more-steady momentum of good fortune is greater proficiency with whichever of the Four Leaves of Earning Serendipity—(1) seeing, (2) sowing, (3) growing, and (4) sharing—you are currently weak. The book has taught you the specifics of this endeavor on an individual level. Yet I must remind you that a momentum of good fortune can be accomplished outside of your skills alone.

If you own a company or play an executive role in a company, you can create and sustain a momentum of good fortune by hiring people proficient in each of the Four Leaves—in particular, by hiring people proficient in the leaves with which you are not or which are not covered in your responsibilities.

Perhaps you are strong in seeing and sowing but somewhat lacking in growing and sharing. Who will you hire to grow your seeds and share your company's harvest? You must answer these questions well.

Or perhaps you are the visionary (seer) with a big heart for sharing the harvest. Is this not common of the leaders of today's nonprofits? You must hire people gifted in sowing and growing the seeds of opportunity in the fields before your company. Don't make the mistake of merely hiring people like you. Compassion is key in this world of business, but it is only emotion if not followed by application. Hiring only fellow seers and sharers will make it difficult for you to sustain a momentum of good fortune.

If you are a worker climbing the ladder of your organization or industry, focus on applying the particular leaves with which you are most gifted, and then associate yourself with Leaders and Lifters who possess the complementary leaves. If, for instance, you possess strength in sowing and growing seeds, endeavor to work *for* a leader who sees with circular vision and *with* coworkers or an organization with a passion for sharing the harvest. To strategically associate yourself with the complementary leaves will not only increase your propensity for good fortune, it will also teach you to be a more-complete serendipiter—we give to and receive much from those with whom we work. In the end, if you possess all Four Leaves of Earning Serendipity via personal skills or strategic collaboration, you will accomplish much that is in your head and on your heart. For additional help on following this path, review the Resources for Serendipiters at the end of the book or go to www.earningserendipity.com.

If your SQ is 31–35 . . .

You possess proficiency with at least one of the Four Leaves of Earning Serendipity. Your strength lies in the skill(s) with which you scored the closest to the maximum score. To boost your ability to sustain good fortune in your work, you must first focus on maximizing your best skill. This will initially set you apart as a primary seer, sower, grower, or sharer in your workplace. This is the first requirement to becoming a serendipiter.

Your SQ is in the most common range of people who employers would call "quality employees." Like the majority of those in this range, you likely don't lack confidence that you can find and keep a job—and even do that job well. Thus, work ethic is probably not a major hurdle for you. In the least, you are likely a self-motivated person, a good sower. When given a job to do, you get it done.

The question you must ask yourself now is whether you possess another skill that is not being utilized in your current workplace. I have found that most who score in this range possess but do not utilize another of the Four Leaves. In what other category did you score high? Do you possess an abundance of circular vision but have little opportunity to put it to use? Do you possess a heart for sharing the harvest but have little influence over company strategy and policy? These are tough questions to answer truly but ones that must be addressed if you are ever to expand your ability to sustain a momentum of good fortune.

I have found that most in this SQ range rarely sustain a momentum of good fortune for the long term because they do not put themselves in a position to utilize or collaborate with more than one leaf. While most in this range possess more than one, their positions require them to solely be a seer, sower, grower, or sharer. This—combined with an inability to leverage complementary leaves that coworkers, colleagues, or bosses possess—results in a reliance on the good fortune only one leaf can create. This will not be enough for you to earn a perpetual harvest. You will win some and lose some in perpetuity.

You are likely stuck in a place where good fortune and misfortune come in somewhat equal and unpredictable spurts. I have found the following to be the career positions in which this often occurs:

- Common Seers who get stuck: executives, small business owners, artists
- Common Sowers who get stuck: salespeople, investors, accountants
- Common Growers who get stuck: managers, marketers, advertisers
- Common Sharers who get stuck: executive assistants, service professionals, nonprofit workers

These who are stuck utilizing only one leaf have jobs that require them to do just that—jobs that pay them to do just that. The good news is that if your company has hired well and possesses people who utilize the other three leaves, you are working for a company with more good fortune than misfortune. This realization may change your opinion of the place at which you work. It is a valuable thing to work for a company that sustains a momentum of good fortune, especially if it is led by an individual who understands the need to continually see, sow, grow, and share opportunities. The only question you must ask is this: Is it enough to be secured by the good fortune of this company?

If your answer is yes, you must only concentrate on maximizing your proficiency with the leaf for which you are responsible. This will ensure that you remain in a position surrounded by perpetual harvest.

If your answer is no—if you would prefer to have more control over your fortune than what your position allows—then you must begin to work toward a position or environment that utilizes the magic of more than one leaf. The wisest path to take is toward a position that requires the proficiency of another skill in which you scored high— perhaps your second highest score. You must take this path whether it winds through your current position or another, or in your current company or another. This is the only way to expand your harvest and increase your momentum of good fortune. To build additional skills, review the Resources for Serendipiters at the end of this book or go to www.earningserendipity.com.

If your SQ is 26–30 . . .

You possess an average SQ in your work. This means you have likely had your lucky streaks and unlucky streaks in somewhat random proportion throughout your working life. While you are not entirely a slave to chance, you are likely doing little to see and seize the good fortune available in your career. To improve your ability to earn serendipity, you must first narrow in on the one leaf that you possess in greatest measure. Are you most naturally a seer, sower, grower, or sharer? You must begin to create a momentum of good fortune from the leaf that comes most naturally for you because it is this skill that you are able to develop most rapidly.

If you are most naturally a seer, you are likely in a position of leadership or headed in that direction. Yet because you did not score well on the quiz, it is likely that you are prone to dreaming and not doing. Perhaps you have great ideas with potential for an immense harvest but you don't have the time or entrepreneurial temperament to sow those ideas into real soil. Perhaps your hands remain clean and you attempt to lead from the authority your position lends you.

176

While this might meet quotas and keep you employed, it will do little to create a momentum of good fortune. Without the effect of other leaves on your side, your fortune will remain unpredictable. If those who work with you and for you do not possess a high SQ—which we might assume from your score is the case—your harvest is limited. The most natural first step to creating and sustaining a momentum of good fortune from this place is to ensure that your work is linked with sowers who can plant your ideas into real soil.

I would be remiss if I didn't also tell you that you must associate yourself with growers and sharers, but I have found that those in your standing must first create the foundation of good fortune by beginning to apply their top skill. This starts by putting your ideas to the test of soil. Once you begin to see your seeds springing to life, you will know which ideas have merit, and you will thus more readily find the motivation and means to grow them, through your own resources or those of others.

There is of course one final measure by which your good fortune must be sustained and that is through the sharing of your harvest. I will not explain this in great detail here because this skill is discussed in detail in chapter 4. Furthermore, I do not want to give you reason to misprioritize your steps. If you are prone to dreaming and not doing, it is better that you not consider how you will share your harvest until a harvest is nearly tangible before you. For now, focus on utilizing your top leaf and then associating yourself with those of the first three leaves that are next in the progression: seeing, sowing, and then growing. Remember that all momentum of good fortune begins with seeing and then sowing the best seeds of opportunity before you. For additional help on following this path, review the Resources for Serendipiters at the end of this book or go to www.earningserendipity.com.

If your SQ is 21–25 . . .

You possess a low inclination to earn good fortune in your career. This means you have likely had more unlucky streaks than lucky streaks. It also means that you tend to be someone who would rather wait and see what happens than someone who makes things happen through both failure and success. For this reason, you tend to be somewhat enslaved to the sway of your circumstances with either untapped skill or untapped desire for doing what is necessary to improve your work. To make the best use of all that you have read thus far, focus solely on strengthening the one leaf in which you scored the closest to the maximum score. If you have two or more leaves with the same top score, then choose the one that is most natural for you.

Because you have some ground to cover, you must first become proficient at one skill in order to wield some initial control over your circumstances—something that is not currently at your disposal. While it is likely you will not yet be able to seize all the best opportunities available to you, by making yourself specifically useful to an organization or cause you will give yourself some stability from which you can begin to develop other skills and pursue better opportunities within your current company or elsewhere.

You must not lose hope in this place, but it is imperative that you accept responsibility for your actions of the past and take control of your actions from here forward. Develop your strongest leaf first and secure your workplace position. With that stability begin employing the Earning Serendipity Methodology in your everyday tasks. Use strategic associations with coworkers, colleagues, friends, and family who can help you see, sow, and grow in greater measure. In time, you will begin to realize a momentum of good fortune that will yield a harvest for you to share. Take care to follow through with this final step. It will be tempting for you—having not reaped a harvest of good fortune before—to hoard the harvest for yourself. Do this and you will be more prone than those with higher SQs to return to where you are now. Share your first harvest and you will increase it all the more. For additional help on following this path, review the Resources for Serendipiters at the end of this book or go to www.earningserendipity.com.

If your SQ is 20 or below . . .

You are likely someone others believe to be unlucky. You unfortunately possess no inclination to see and seize good fortune in your career, but your situation is not without hope. You are still someone for whom this book was written. To make the best use of what you've learned, focus on learning from someone you know (and preferably work with) who appears to possess a measure of good fortune. Observe the leaves this one puts to use on a regular basis and take in how it affects this person's momentum. As you observe, begin considering which leaf seems most appealing to you. This is likely the leaf that you possess in greatest measure right now. Your next step is to begin strengthening this skill through application within your current work environment. As this one skill becomes second nature to you, you will begin to see how it affects your level of good fortune. It is likely that one of the first evidences of good fortune is an increased measure of stability in your workplace. This is not to be taken lightly because it affords you the time to begin putting the entire Earning Serendipity Methodology to use.

Use current relationships and strategic associations with coworkers and colleagues to help you see, sow, and grow in greater measure. In time, you will begin to increase your momentum of good fortune and eventually yield a harvest to share. Follow through with this final step. Share your first harvest and you will increase it all the more. History has proven it to be so. Before long, others will begin to see you as one of the lucky ones. For additional help in jump-starting your proficiency with the Four Leaves of Earning Serendip-ity, review the Resources for Serendipiters at the end of this book or go to www.earningserendipity.com.

The Serendipiter's Quiz

The following quiz is designed to help those with SQs of 26 or higher determine whether their efforts to move to the next level of earning serendipity are hindered by core beliefs about success, failure, and good fortune. For best results, do not overthink the questions. Read each one and its subsequent answers only twice and then choose your answer with a top-of-mind response. I have found that those who overanalyze the questions and answers end up with inaccuracies in their scores. The strength of these questions is that they test inclinations that will naturally affect your typical approaches to any particular endeavor—in this case your endeavor to see, sow, grow, and share the opportunities all around you.

1. **Do you believe in chance?**

    A—Not at all
    B—Doesn't matter
    C—Somewhat
    D—Definitely

2. **Can you control whether you are a fortunate or an unfortunate person?**

    A—Not at all
    B—Not sure
    C—Somewhat
    D—Definitely

3. **How much do others influence your life experience?**

    A—Not at all
    B—Very little
    C—That depends
    D—A lot

4. **How much does your past affect your present?**

    A—Not at all
    B—Very little
    C—That depends
    D—A lot

5. **Do you believe you are meant for a certain life?**

    A—Not at all
    B—Not sure
    C—Somewhat
    D—Yes

6. **Do you believe in fortunate accidents?**

    A—Not at all
    B—Somewhat
    C—That depends
    D—Yes

7. **Do certain missed opportunities come back to you?**

    A—No
    B—Rarely
    C—Sometimes
    D—Often

8. **Do good things come to those who wait?**

   A—Never

   B—Rarely

   C—Usually

   D—Always

9. **Can failure and misfortune be good?**

   A—Never

   B—Rarely

   C—Sometimes

   D—Always

10. **Are lucky people successful?**

   A—Not at all

   B—Rarely

   C—Sometimes

   D—Yes

The Serendipiter's Quiz

....

Point system for your Advanced Serendipity Quotient (ASQ):

1A = 3 points

1B = 4 points

1C = 1 point

1D = 2 points

2A = 1 point

2B = 2 points

2C = 3 points

2D = 4 points

3A = 3 points

3B = 2 points

3C = 1 point

3D = 4 points

4A = 1 point

4B = 3 points

4C = 2 points

4D = 4 points

5A = 2 points

5B = 3 points

5C = 1 point

5D = 4 points

6A = 2 points

6B = 4 points

6C = 1 point

6D = 3 points

7A = 1 point

7B = 4 points

7C = 3 points

7D = 2 points

8A = 3 points

8B = 4 points

8C = 2 points

8D = 1 point

9A = 1 point

9B = 2 points

9C = 3 points

9D = 4 points

10A = 4 points

10B = 3 points

10C = 2 points

10D = 1 point

The Serendipiter's Quiz

If your ASQ is 36–40 . . .

In general, your core beliefs will not hinder you from optimizing your ability to earn serendipity. You are open-minded about seeing and seizing opportunities in success and failure. While you are not thrilled about mistakes and the potential misfortune that might come to you outside your control, you are motivated to find seeds of opportunity within both. Additionally, you are one who believes that what happens to a person is more often a result of cause and effect than mere happenstance. These core beliefs will make it much easier for you to increase your proficiency with the Four Leaves of Earning Serendipity. In short, there are few, if any, psychological obstacles between where you are now and where you can be with an increased ability to earn serendipity.

Continue to apply the advice given in your workplace serendipity quiz results and you will continue to elevate your probability for good fortune in your work. This is not to say you will never experience misfortune. It is to say that misfortune will become less and less likely because it will be increasingly less a result of your actions or beliefs. The Resources for Serendipiters at the end of this book, as well as information at www.earningserendipity.com, will help you along the way.

If your ASQ is 31–35 . . .

Your core beliefs should not pose a major problem once you see the effect of applying the Four Leaves of Earning Serendipity. You are likely a "see it to believe it" type person rather than an emotional decision maker. Perhaps we might say you are more geared toward core beliefs based on tangible experiences than core beliefs based on senses. There is great value in this until it keeps you from seeing and believing the universal intangibles all around you.

Once you begin experiencing the tangible effects of seeing, sowing, growing, and sharing opportunities, it is likely you will begin to trust that much of what we call good and bad fortune is merely a result of cause and effect. In sum, one's fortune has more to do with an ability or inability to see and seize opportunity than mere happenstance. While you do not believe we are mere creatures of fate, your primary obstacle will likely be a psychological bent toward not knowing what determines our fortunes. This can be overcome to an extent by diligence and hard work. But when it comes to reaching the highest potential in your work, you must learn to trust the intangible advantages that great opportunities present before those opportunities pass you by.

In the end, you will not maximize good fortune in your work until you learn to see and seize opportunities before they offer you tangible returns. The best way to do so is to continue seeing, sowing, growing, and sharing the great opportunities currently before you. I have found that the more you see the tangible returns of earning serendipity, the more you will believe that you have much to do with the good fortune in your work. For more ideas on how to increase your propensity to earn good fortune, see the Resources for Serendipiters at the end of this book or visit www.earningserendipity.com.

If your ASQ is 30 or below . . .

Until you alter your core beliefs, they will hinder you from proficiently applying the Four Leaves of Earning Serendipity to your work. This does not mean you will not experience good fortune. It is certain that you possess proficiency with at least one of the leaves and this will bring you some good fortune—more so if you have surrounded yourself with others who possess complementary leaves. Still, your ability in and of yourself to affect your fortune will not make dramatic increases until you are intrinsically motivated by a belief that the opportunities you see and seize (as well as those you miss) can dramatically alter your good fortune in your work. This is often the result of a core belief that you cannot control much of the misfortune that befalls you. Until you learn to believe otherwise, you will remain ineffective at seeing the opportunities inherent in failure and misfortune. Perhaps negative emotions get the best of you in such circumstances. This can hinder you, but your passion can be immensely valuable if reigned and guided.

As you begin applying the Four Leaves in your work, begin taking note of the areas of your life that are not as you'd like. Are these circumstances a result of mere happenstance? Or are they the result of an opportunity that you did not see or that you failed to seize? Hindsight can be a candid teacher if we are willing and wise enough to learn from her. If you will begin to increase your ability to earn serendipity in your work, you must begin to see, sow, grow, and share the harvest of opportunities in more than the obvious places around you. There is much you can learn from the immigrant and the entrepreneur who find more good fortune in the obscure places where few think to look. For more ideas on how to increase your propensity to earn good fortune, see the Resources for Serendipiters at the end of this book or go to www.earningserendipity.com.

RESOURCES FOR SERENDIPITERS

At EarningSerendipity.com, you'll find critical resources that will enhance your efforts to improve your Serendipity Quotient (SQ) and help you connect with other serendipiters around the globe. From EarningSerendipity. com, you can connect to Serendipiters.com, an online network that breeds and guides the development of socially conscious innovators and establishes a common ground for innovation across fields, careers, and borders. Because serendipiters are socially conscious, Serendipiters.com will unite members in their efforts to propel economic development locally, regionally, nationally, and globally.

The sites will offer the following core tools of education and enlightenment:

- Virtual training and webinars
- Innovation-based education (through alliances with universities, corporations, and small-business owners worldwide)
- Mentoring groups
- Resource materials, such as articles and case studies
- Videos, blogs, and RSS communication tools
- Tools to support the development of multicultural groups
- Country-specific modules that allow members to find relevant and local resources

My hope is that through these resources, we can build a strong community of people who are devoted to improving the economic futures of their communities in sustainable ways.

In addition, the Glenn Llopis Group has launched a dynamic new online forum. More than just a blog, *The Thresher,* available at www.Thresher Online.com, is an assembly of luminaries devoted to cultivating ideas and sharing the harvest. Each day, a new daily topic is presented to our contributor base of best-selling authors, academicians, business leaders, and other leading voices from all walks of life. They are given the opportunity to post their thoughts, and you are given the opportunity to respond.

The Thresher is devoted to vibrant discussion among smart, opinionated people. And this means you! Log on today and start expanding your horizons. Sometimes you'll agree, sometimes you won't. Either way, we want to hear from you!

NOTES

1   Proverbs 13:20, *New International Bible.*

2   Adapted from a 2004 article by Research Machines plc and posted at
    http://encyclopedia.farlex.com/Fallow-ground.

3   Proverbs 27:14, *New International Bible.*

4   Bronwyn Lance, "The Economic Impact of Immigrants," May 2000,
    www.adti.net.

5   Proverbs 13:20, *New International Bible.*

ACKNOWLEDGMENTS

As the words of this book were born at my birth, I technically have everyone to thank for its outcome. But as I begin to consider the Earning Serendipity Methodology—what it means to business and represents to society—I can only assimilate a select few who have traveled with me through the ebbs and flows of my journey and never stopped believing.

I must first thank my immediate family:

While it is my father to whom I have dedicated this book, it is my mother, Jenny Llopis, who deserves equal credit. She is a serendipiter in her own right. An only child who lost her parents before adolescence, my mother is as resilient as one comes. She is timeless and beautiful, and she taught me to respect the world regardless of color, race, educational, or economic differences. She managed a family with the highest of standards and viewed "love thy neighbor" as a necessity. She taught me to love people without fear or consequence. She also provided me with the wisdom to share the harvest plentifully. Thank you, Mom—I love you with all of my heart. You are the best.

My older brother, Eric Llopis, is one of a kind. Now a top executive at Pepsi Bottling Group, he can be best characterized as my reality check, the one who always kept me grounded when I was prone to unrealistic dreams. It is always good to have one like my brother in your life. I love you, Eric, and I am so proud of you and your accomplishments in business and life. You, your beautiful wife, Taj, and the kids (Marina, Isabel, and Nicolaus) have inspired me through it all.

And then, of course, I must thank the love of my life—Annette. You, my Dear, are the ultimate. After forty-two years of believing that the right woman would enter my life and open my heart forever, you "serendipitously" arrived. You have given me more than I could have ever expected. You are the master of unconditional love, and the lessons I have learned from you about relationships deserve their own book. You have fueled my life, and as we now embark upon our dreams, this book will serve as our map that we will pass down through the generations to come. I am the most fortunate man, and God shared his harvest with me when you became my bride. I love you more than words can say.

I would like now to devote some space to my special friends, serendipiters in their own right. Though I have not spoken to some of them in quite some time, their impact in my life is nonetheless significant. They too deserve to be acknowledged here.

- Armando Azarloza: Your leadership is contagious and our friendship profound. You make Cubans proud.
- Mr. Gong Jin Choi: My international serendipiter and South Korean brother.
- Brent Cole: Your discovery made this all a reality. Your writing talent is a gift from God. We will always be connected.
- Cathy Connolly: Our relationship is one of a kind, and your family will forever be connected to my life's work.
- Victoria Cunningham: You took a chance and we made Luna Rossa a reality. Thank you and your kids for all of your devotion.
- Mark DeBellis: You have always been like a brother to me. You have been my most special mentor, and your wisdom will forever be a part of my teachings for generations to come.
- Gilbert De Cardenas Sr.: You gave me the added strength to believe in my vision and shared the wisdom that allowed my immigrant perspective to come into full use.
- Jim and Marnie Duenas: The first community of serendipiters. You are special to me and you know it!
- Walter Fawcett: May this project optimize you and take you to where you belong.
- The Greenleaf Team: For believing in the project and for your dedication and devotion to the message. I will forever be grateful.
- William A. Hamad: You taught me that traditional skills have become commoditized. That people are blinded to identifying what is "great talent." Because of you, I have unleashed my message internationally and am "fishing where the fish swim."
- Steve Handley: You gave this project sustained momentum and life. You are a powerful role model and an incredible talent.
- Karl Hansen: For always supporting me during the uncertain times and making the journey special.
- Ernie Hicks: For guiding the financial wisdom of my ventures.
- Steve Howell: You were one of the first to listen to my boyish rants yet took the time to breed a businessman.
- Vern Hunt: You have always been a spiritual foundation and I will forever be grateful.
- Jeremiah J. Jacks: For allowing me to trust in partnerships again— thank you for your grace.

- David Jones: You have always been a special part of our family and my journey. Thank you for your unconditional love and devotion.
- Meg LaBorde: You are so talented, and yet not even fully blossomed. Watch out, world, when you are.
- Brandon Lester, Michael Binder, and Tomer Baron: My interns today, tomorrow's leaders.
- Mike Loudon: For discovering the seed of my potential and letting it flourish.
- Lee Lubin: You fought some battles with me and taught me the legal system. Through this journey we learned about the depth of our special friendship; one that few experience in life.
- Familia Madrazo Placeres: We made things happen even when we weren't quite ready! I thank you for your love and devotion.
- Rich Melcombe: Your incredible insights liberated my thinking and expanded my abilities to new heights.
- Debbie Moysychyn: You are the ultimate role model for women. They will lead the world someday, and you will lead them.
- Orlando Ortega: You represent the power of circular vision. You are a gift to society.
- Todd Peterson: You taught me the value of hard work while at UCLA. Now you're a successful surgeon and role model for others. You deserve it.
- Vince Poscente: You gave me the keys to your experience with no limits. What a gift.
- David Robertshaw: Thank you for embracing the immigrant perspective.
- Tony Robinson: For giving me my first career break and coaching me through the process.
- Roland Schertenleib: For giving serendipiters life and meaning, and for giving this project visual relevancy and purpose.
- Steve Schooler: For taking the chance when the chance didn't exist.
- Kevin Small: You are a servant leader and innovator. You will help change the world.
- Stephen J. Smith: Your enthusiasm, dedication, and intelligence are incredible. It is now your time to shine; may this movement help you get there.
- Gregory Sulak: My college roommate who came to realize that my crazy ideas made sense.

- UCLA: For believing in a young man from Azusa, California.
- Rob Ukropina: For taking the time to be a real friend and opening new doors for discovery.
- Bill Waldo: For your time, wisdom, and deep belief in the project.
- Adlai Wertman: You are the appointed leader of the Serendipiter Community. Your brotherly love will forever be valued and respected.
- Mr. Larry Winzenread: Believe, Achieve, Conceive. You are the ultimate Rhino!

GLENN LLOPIS GROUP (GLG)
PRODUCT AND SERVICE OFFERINGS
FROM SERENDIPITY UNIVERSITY

1. Keynote Speaking

"Glenn's message is sure to strike home with today's young professionals and entrepreneurs. A workplace that adopts and espouses the principles of management that Glenn teaches is almost guaranteed a leg up with the best minds of this new generation."

—Dr. P. K. Shukla, director of the Leatherby Center for Entrepreneurship and Business Ethics, Argyros School of Business and Economics, Chapman University

In the Earning Serendipity Keynote Series, Glenn has expanded on the lessons of *Earning Serendipity* to create a compelling series of presentations around each of the book's main themes. Intended for corporate and academic audiences alike, Glenn's lectures bring a fascinating sense of history to the stage, demonstrating the practical application of the ES Methodology through the lives of such storied successes as Thomas Edison, Henry Ford, Warren Buffett, Bill Gates, and more. Glenn's entertaining yet informative style instills audiences with a powerful, take-charge message.

Each lecture in the series is suitable as a stand-alone presentation, and bookings are available for the whole series or single lectures. In addition, GLG can customize presentations to meet your organization's specific goals. For more information, please contact:

Melissa Brown Publicity
8605 Santa Monica Blvd. #20540
Los Angeles, CA 90069
www.MelissaBrownPublicity.com
Info@MelissaBrownPublicity.com
Phone: 714.453.9186